16.75

# TEACHING MENTALLY RETARDED CHILDREN THROUGH MUSIC

*By*

**M. K. Hoshizaki**

**CHARLES C THOMAS** • **PUBLISHER**
*Springfield • Illinois • U.S.A.*

*Published and Distributed Throughout the World by*
CHARLES C THOMAS • PUBLISHER
2600 South First Street
Springfield, Illinois, 62717, U.S.A.

© *1983 by* CHARLES C THOMAS • PUBLISHER

ISBN 0-398-04739-1

Library of Congress Catalog Card Number: 82-10285

*Printed in the United States of America*
*CU-R-1*

*Library of Congress Cataloging in Publication Data*

Hoshizaki, M. K. (Masami, K.)
    Teaching mentally retarded children through music.

    Bibliography: p.
    Includes indexes.
    1. Music therapy.   2. Mentally handicapped
children--Education.   I. Title.
ML3920.H67   1983        371.92'803        82-10285
ISBN 0-398-04739-1

# PREFACE

I WALKED into a classroom for educable retarded children one morning and found myself in a scene from a teacher's nightmare. The quiet children were lost in their own worlds and seemed unaware of the commotion surrounding them. One boy chased another through the room, both of them banging into furniture and knocking things down as they ran. Other children yelled at each other as if their lives depended upon being heard. Several roamed aimlessly in the aisles. One trio of boys stood at the activity table pulling things apart and throwing the pieces on the table or at each other. After a while, the teacher, a young man not long out of college, took two of the boys by the neck and left the room, returning a few minutes later alone.

One group of children sat patiently at a table where the teacher listened to a girl labor through a long, slow, painful rendition of the twos table. Having stated that two times one equals two, the child continued, "two times two equals. . . ." There followed a long pause while she, using her fingers, added two to her first answer. When she finally decided that two times two equals four, she began the trying process of adding two to four in order to determine the answer to two times three. I did not see how the teacher could stand there and listen to the distressing performance; I was in agony.

When the girl had managed to plow through the twos table, the teacher came to speak to me. "Boy," he said, "I wish I were back in college. Things were easy then. You can *have* this class."

In the room next door, I found another young teacher sitting with three children before a chalkboard playing a language arts game. Everyone seemed to be busy. One girl began motioning me to sit in the chair in front of her. I hesitated, not wanting the girl to leave her work and become involved in conversation with me. However, she continued to make signs at me to sit down, and I decided that it would be better to accept her invitation. I need not have worried about distracting her; she introduced herself and the girl sitting next to her, then returned to her work and did not say another word to me.

At recess time, the teacher insisted that everyone go outside. When they were gone she explained, "At the beginning of the year, all this class wanted was to have recess. I found that what I'd been taught to do didn't work, so I had to forget everything I learned in college and start all over using my own methods and making up games and materials for the class to use. The kids have really responded. They like what they are doing so much that they don't even want to go out for recess anymore."

As a teacher and, for a time, as an observer for an educational assessment service, I have seen hundreds of teachers of all kinds. It is interesting that I should have found two teachers in the same school who so clearly illustrate what I believe to be the most important of the elements that determine the value of a teacher—the ability to learn from students and to think creatively.

Isaac Asimov describes the perfect teaching situation in these words: "The quintessence of education is to have one student facing one teacher. If you are the student, let it be a teacher who knows your strengths and weaknesses, your interests and boredoms, your conventionalities and peculiarities; a teacher who can pay attention to *you* and who, most important of all, can learn from you and use that learning to teach you the more efficiently" (Asimov, 1978).

Those who work with mentally retarded children will surely agree that Asimov's statement is even truer when applied to their own pupils. However, it is extremely difficult to be a good teacher to people who have few strengths and many weaknesses, limited interests and countless boredoms, numerous ingrained conventionalities and widely diversified peculiarities. In addition, most teachers of the mentally retarded must try to teach children on a one-to-one basis in one-to-eight or one-to-fifteen situations.

The teacher who is placed in such a position does not find educational philosophy, statistics, educational psychology, the history of education, or even courses in methods to be very helpful. Instead of studying education, the teacher must now study the students to learn what each of them needs and then find ways to meet those needs.

The music specialist is a teacher who uses music in a manner calculated to help fulfill the needs of the students. In this book, I have not given prescriptions for teachers to follow, for I do not know the pupils with whom they work. Instead, I have emphasized the importance of careful study, which is necessary in order to determine what each child needs to learn, when he is ready to learn, and how he can learn most efficiently. I believe that teachers who thoughtfully observe individual children will have ideas that are more useful than any specific measures I might recommend.

Although the thoughts presented here apply both to educable and trainable children, I have illustrated most of them with very simple activities and songs for the sake of teachers of the severely retarded, who need more teaching materials than other teachers and are generally able to find less. Teachers of educable classes should not feel the need for more examples as the intention of this book is to show *how* not *what*.

To avoid the constant use of *he or she*, *him or her*, and *his or her*, I have chosen to use masculine pronouns in referring to teachers. The message of this book is the same for all teachers, male and female: never be satisfied with knowing *what* a child cannot do; find out *why* he cannot do it. Good teaching begins when we tackle the reason behind a child's failure to learn.

# ACKNOWLEDGMENTS

THE idea of employing music as a teaching aid was totally unknown to me when I first began working with retarded children at the Lochland School in Geneva, New York. It was Florence H. Stewart, founder of the school, who interested me in exploring the possibilities of using music not as an adjunct to but as an integral part of the teaching program. I owe much to Miss Stewart for her guidance in my earliest efforts and for the encouragement she has provided through the years.

I am also indebted to Natalie Perry, author of *Teaching the Mentally Retarded Child*, who taught me to observe children in order to determine the reasons for their learning problems and find ways of helping them resolve or get around their problems.

I want to thank Nancy Brown, Terry Roberts, and Marley Sackheim, three principals whose cooperation made it possible for me to try new ideas and materials with our classes.

Parents in various schools have given me help for which I am truly grateful. Some of them expertly constructed equipment for me, precisely following what may at times have seemed rather weird specifications. Other parents gave me a better understanding of retarded children and their families by talking freely to me about their children and their problems.

My family has been most understanding and supportive. I thank my husband, George, for the many hours he spent helping in the preparation of the manuscript. My daughters, Janice and Eunice, put up with me in the days when they felt that "Mommy is mean and crabby because of her dumb old book," and, more recently, have been valued consultants and assistants. I am grateful to Steve Boston for his advice and assistance in preparing the musical examples, and I hope he believes that Eunice did not marry him because I needed his help.

Most of all I thank the children I have known, for it is they who taught me how to teach.

# CONTENTS

# TEACHING MENTALLY RETARDED CHILDREN THROUGH MUSIC

Chapter 1

# INTRODUCTION

THE training of the mentally retarded is a specialty requiring special knowledge, special equipment, and special techniques. The purpose of this book is to acquaint the reader with the special technique of applying music as a tool in teaching retarded children. Everything discussed in these pages has to do with the development of muscular control, the development of language and speech, self-help training, emotional and social development, or the reinforcement of learning—all with the help of music. Our purpose is to show how to incorporate the fun of music into learning activities in order to make them more interesting and entertaining. We are not concerned with music education or with music as recreation.

This does not imply a disapproval of music education for the retarded, nor does it mean that retarded children should not have music just for fun. There are many books on music education and on recreational activities with music. There is also an increasing amount of material on the education of the mentally retarded. However, there is very little to be found regarding functional music in the training of retarded children. Our intent, therefore, is to concentrate on those skills, both basic and academic, that the schools are trying to teach and to find ways in which music can help in the teaching.

## WHY MUSIC?

Most of us have heard at one time or another that music is the universal language, the idea being that individuals who cannot communicate through the use of a common tongue can still enjoy music together. An analysis of the kinds of people who like music will show that music bridges much more than differences in spoken language.

The serious student of music enjoys the various techniques composers use to bring together tones and rhythms to produce pleasing effects; he derives satisfaction from interpreting vocal or instrumental music; or he may express himself in original compositions. The musically uneducated person may not know the names of chords, the style of a particular composer, or the form of a composition, but he can still be happy listening to or humming along with a recording or strumming or blowing an instrument.

The intellectually gifted or highly educated person may find much pleasure in music. The person who is intellectually limited or has never been to school can have as much fun with music as the individual with several advanced degrees.

It takes talent to give an artistic rendition of a vocal or instrumental number, but it takes no talent to enjoy listening to someone else make music. Many persons who have no musical ability get much pleasure from singing or dancing, though their listeners and dancing partners may suffer terribly. Even uninterested or inattentive people may find that music intrudes beyond the conscious level of hearing to evoke a visible physical response such as nodding or foot tapping.

So music can reach the musically educated and the musically uneducated, the literate and the illiterate, the brilliant and the dull, the talented and the untalented, and even people who do not listen.

Severely retarded children, therefore, are able to make good use of music. Most of them are fond of music because they can listen to it, move to it, play instruments with it, sing along with it, or play games to it. They can enjoy listening to music even though they do not understand spoken language. They can sing a tune without being able to speak. They can physically respond to musical rhythms even if their coordination is poor. They find it easier to attend to music than to concentrate on other things. For these reasons, musically treated learning experiences are particularly effective for retarded children.

Almost every human being is capable of producing and responding to music because music is a natural form of expression. The basic elements of music—pitch and rhythm—are also the basic elements in human expression.

The infant cries to express discomfort; he coos and laughs to show pleasure. As he grows older, the child learns to organize his vocal sounds into patterns we call speech, and he uses melodic inflections and variations in speed and volume to add color to his speech and make it more expressive.

Rhythmic expression comes through bodily movement. Consider, for example, the jumping and clapping that show delight or the slow, swaying motion that depicts sorrow. Much of our communication is a combination of melody and rhythm—speech and gestures.

By combining its pleasure-giving qualities with dull, everyday activities or with difficult tasks, we can make music perform many useful functions, and we see it at work every day. Television and radio advertisers often use music in presenting their commercial messages, and even the listener who is irritated by the asinine ditties may at times find himself singing them. The music reaches the hearer, and the message sneaks through with it.

Educators have long used the sugarcoating of music to cover up the taste of lessons children do not like. The alphabet, multiplication tables, and rules for safety and good manners are a few things that have been set to music for children.

Dentists and physicians sometimes pipe music into their waiting rooms and offices to relax their patients. Employers who provide periods of music for their workers find that it gives pleasure and improves production as well.

In these and other ways, music makes ordinary activities more enjoyable or less unpleasant for people of all ages, abilities, and backgrounds. Most people can attend to their tasks or keep themselves under control even though music is not provided for them. Retarded children, however, often have short attention spans, and they may need to have their interests aroused and sustained by something outside of the tasks they are to perform. Music, with its wide appeal and its power to communicate at levels other than the intellectual, is one of the most valuable aids in reaching these children.

## MUSIC FOR ALL

From time to time, we hear that some retarded children, especially those with brain damage, should never have music because they become overstimulated and/or confused by it. If a child becomes terribly excited and hyperactive upon hearing music, we ought to try music that is quieter both in volume and in rhythm. If this does not help, we should still not rule music out of his life, for there are probably many musical activities he can enjoy without getting all upset.

Music can be broken down into three broad parts—melody, harmony, and rhythm. Each of these components, apart from the others, can provide satisfying musical experiences. Children who cannot handle a combination of all three may find pleasure in just one or perhaps two of the three. A child who is disturbed by one aspect of music may find a great deal of enjoyment in another.

Some children are distracted by melody and cannot get the meaning of the words they sing. It would be a mistake to deprive these children of all music. Instead of singing, they might recite the lyrics of a song, either individually or in chorus. Instrumental music that has no accompanying words may be another good substitute for singing, and bodily rhythms done either to instrumental accompaniment or to rhythmic speech can give these children many enjoyable musical moments.

Children who are confused by harmony can use music that concentrates on melody and rhythm. Children like this might have fun picking out tunes on the song bells, xylophone, psaltery, and tuned bells, or they might sing to the accompaniment of such a melodic instrument. Beating or tapping out rhythms on percussion instruments is another activity that omits the element of harmony in music.

Then, there are children who are upset by strong rhythms. The answer for these children, of course, is the avoidance of highly rhythmic music and the adherence to very basic, unexciting rhythms. Finding chords on an autoharp to accompany a melody, or experimenting with tonal effects using tuned bells or blocks or different kinds of drums are examples of musical things children can do without getting involved in exciting rhythms.

If a child becomes confused or upset when asked to do two things such as marching and beating drums to music at the same time, the sensible teacher will ask him to do one or the other, not both, or he will let the child sing or just listen to music. A child with neurological impairment does not necessarily have to be deprived of music altogether.*

If a child does not seem to like music or if he seems unable to function with music, it is our responsibility to determine exactly what it is about music that disturbs him. We should then try to eliminate the disturbing element and look for musical activities that the child can enjoy. It is a rare child who cannot enjoy music at all.

---

* If a doctor or therapist has specifically stated that a particular child should have no music, the school should probably comply with that recommendation.

## WHAT METHOD?

Any teacher who is capable of teaching retarded children should also be able to run a music program for them. Many teachers, however, are afraid to try music with any class, normal or retarded, while music specialists feel uneasy about practicing their specialty with retarded children. Perhaps this is why teachers and specialists are often anxious to find a specific musical method to follow. We have often been asked, "Do you use the Orff method?" and we think it important to answer that question before we go any further.

Carl Orff's ideas are meant to work toward creative musicianship by encouraging musical expression through bodily movement and musical improvisation. In the words of Harris Danziger, "What the Orff approach provides is a bridge between the earliest, spontaneous musical expression of a child and the time when he is ready to undertake the study of a musical instrument" (Ewen, 1969).

The purpose of the Orff program is to teach music. Our purpose is to use music as a teaching tool. The Orff approach stresses creativity in students. We want to inspire creativity in teachers; experimentation and free expression should be for teachers as well as for students. Those who work with mentally retarded children have to be even more creative than teachers of normal students, as retarded children are not very creative. To make effective use of Orff ideas, the teacher must adapt them for use with children who may be emotionally disturbed, physically handicapped, socially maladjusted, or brain damaged, as well as retarded.

To adopt *one method* to the exclusion of all others is to limit effectiveness. We doubt that our readers would trust a doctor who gives the same treatment for everything from leukemia to ingrown toenails. Have no more faith in a teacher who sticks to one set method in teaching. The truly effective teacher will take the good and reject the bad in every method he can find and then add his own ideas while constantly looking for new things to do and new ways in which to do them.

Fortunately at present, there are no established methods for employing music as a teaching instrument. It is to be hoped that there will never be any method other than one that might be called the Creative Thinking Method. Such a method would not impose uniform equipment or procedures on anyone, and teachers would be free to design materials and activities tailored to the needs of their own pupils.

## HOW TO USE THIS BOOK

Since every group of children differs from all other groups of children and each child differs from all the other children in his group, it is not possible for us to provide musical exercises to completely cover any classroom program. This book only suggests and illustrates things that can be done with music.

It is imperative that the reader be fully cognizant of the effect of personality on learning and teaching. Something that works beautifully with one group or individual may fail with others; one teacher may use a procedure successfully while others cannot make it work, even with the same group of children. The writer's success with a method, therefore, does not insure success for the reader. For this reason, if suggestions given here are not working, the teacher should first make sure that the activities are not too hard for the children. If they are too hard, the obvious answer is to simplify them. If they are within the group's range of understanding and acquired skills, it will be necessary to figure out what is not working and why and then modify the exercises or think up new ones.

The ensuing chapters contain ideas that illustrate the process of diagnosing needs and originating ways of servicing those needs. The intent is to urge creative thinking rather than to supply answers. Teachers and music specialists are asked to keep this in mind and consider ways of helping their own students, even while they read about our experiences.

## Chapter 2

# THE MUSIC ROOM AND ITS EQUIPMENT

FEW of us will ever have the opportunity of supervising the construction of an ideal music room. It is not unlikely that we will conduct music sessions in a classroom cluttered with furniture, in a tiny extra room where children sit squeezed together, or in a gymnasium that seems to swallow up the music and the children too. While we fully realize that this is true, we also feel that each music specialist should have the best possible facilities and equipment, and this chapter is intended to give specialists ideas for improving their present quarters.

The first requisite is that the room be large enough for rhythm work and games. A room that is too small or too narrow forces children to stop running or galloping in order to avoid hitting walls. This prevents them from ever settling into rhythm. In a small room, circle games are crushed; in a long, narrow room they have to be oblong games that soon become disorderly. In a crowded room, it may be necessary to cut out all group activity that requires much movement.

A slippery floor interferes with vigorous rhythm work. Children with good muscle control often enjoy skidding and falling so much that they want to do nothing else, others are so fearful of slipping that they cannot move freely, and still others fall and hurt themselves.

A small rug is useful (and easier to move and store than a tumbling mat) for turning somersaults and rolling on the floor. Most children do not object to the bare floor, but some children and teachers prefer a little padding and less dirt.

Soundproofing of the music room can be a blessing to the rest of the school. Teachers are spared the nuisance of having their classes distracted by the sound of familiar songs or booming drums, while administrative and office personnel get relief from the noise if they are so unfortunate as to be located near the music room.

Protruding cabinets and shelves in a small room should be positioned to take as little usable space as possible. A lock on cabinet

9

doors is useful if there are children who are constantly trying to get at the instruments or other materials. It is also useful for keeping teachers from borrowing instruments and other equipment without permission. Music specialists should not have to go from room to room looking for things that teachers have borrowed and failed to return.

One of the most bothersome things to have in a music room is a large table. Extremely hyperactive children like to climb on top of the table while very young ones often like to sit under it, keeping the teacher busy lifting children off the table or crawling under it after youngsters more agile than he. If there has to be a large table in the room, placing chairs around it makes it harder to climb or to crawl under; at least, it gives the teacher a fighting chance to get to the children before they climb onto or disappear under the table. Another drawback to having a large table in the room is that some children stop to inspect drawers or to bang and rub their instruments on the surface, thus becoming distracted from their original purpose.

A good piano is essential to a good music program and very hard to get. Because it is an expensive item, many schools must either buy an old dilapidated piano or accept an old dilapidated piano as a gift. But whether the piano is good or bad, it must be kept in good repair and in tune if at all possible. The piano should be placed so that the teacher can see the children while he plays it. A teacher who is unable to play with his head turned can try placing a mirror so that he can see the children reflected in it as they move around outside his field of vision. This may not be a satisfactory solution if he is working with children who are greatly interested in studying their own reflections. A teacher who is so fortunate as to have a say in the choice of a piano might request a spinet model. By placing this type of instrument in one corner and sitting with his back to the wall, he can see the entire room across the top of the piano.

Child-size chairs should be provided, though some activities, especially for young children, are more effectively carried out when everyone is sitting on the floor. Most of the work is done in a more orderly manner if the class is seated on chairs. When they sit on the floor, some children tend to crowd together, causing accidental kicks and shoves, which result in complaints, fights, and tears. There are also intentional kicks and shoves that cause complaints, fights, and tears. Then there are those persons who sit facing the wrong way so that they cannot see what is going on.

Having the children sit on chairs makes for better organization. While there are students who move chairs forward or backward or even across the room, most of them leave chairs where they are and use the same one during the entire period. When the program for the day requires much rising and sitting, using chairs saves time as well.

If possible, the chairs should all be of the same kind, as it is sometimes difficult to play games when some people are sitting in small, low chairs while others are perched up high in big chairs. The music specialist whose groups include both very little and very big children may need more than one set of chairs.

A bulletin board or easel on which to display pictures is useful. A music specialist who does not have access to the school picture file needs to have one of his own. Backing pictures with heavy cardboard protects them from being bent and makes them easier to stand on a rack. Finger smudges can be wiped off with a damp cloth if pictures are covered with acetate that is taped into place or with clear adhesive plastic (such as Con-Tact®) that is stuck right onto the picture. This reduces the temptation to say, "Don't touch." The plastic also keeps the picture from tearing; it even makes a picture chew-resistant, but not chewproof.

For children who have not learned to associate pictorial representations with real objects, we may want to have on hand miniature mailboxes, cars, garden tools, clothes, and the like, if we do not have the actual objects in the room.

Pictures can be more useful and lifelike if we "animate" them. A teacher or music specialist who does not have a real goldfish in a bowl can make a picture of a goldfish bowl containing water, rubber cement it to cardboard, and cover it with clear plastic. He can then cement a picture of a goldfish on heavy paper, cover it with clear plastic, cut it out, and stick a small piece of metal (from a bottle cap or food tin) on the back of it. By holding a magnet behind the picture of the bowl, the teacher can make the goldfish "swim" in the water.

Some pictures can be made so that parts can be added to them. One example of this kind of picture shows how to make a snowman. The background—snow-covered ground and sky—is glued to cardboard and covered with acetate or clear plastic. Three snowballs of different sizes are drawn, covered with clear Con-Tact, and cut out.

A piece of two-sided stickum tape is attached to the back of each snowball. As the children sing about making a snowman, the snowballs are stuck to the background—large snowball first, middle-sized one on the first, small one on top. If the real snowman had only two snowballs, the picture would have only two. If the snowman had a hat, scarf, or anything else, the picture can have them too. The detachable pieces may be kept on a piece of wax paper when they are not in use.

Another way to make this type of picture is to rubber cement the picture to cardboard and then cover it with clear plastic wrap such as that used for wrapping food. Make sure that the plastic is stretched smooth; fold the edges over and tape them down to the back of the cardboard. Now glue plastic wrap to the back of each piece of the snowman. If the plastic surfaces are smooth and are kept clean, they will stick to each other making it possible to stick the pieces onto the background as if by magic. This is one time that the annoying tendency of plastic wrap to stick to itself is useful.

If we have to borrow pictures, we can protect them by constructing simple frames for them. One piece of heavy cardboard forms the back of the frame. Taking a second piece of cardboard the same size as the first, cut out a rectangle leaving about two inches all around as a frame. On the back of this piece, glue or tape a sheet of acetate. Place this second piece on the first and join the two along one edge with cloth tape to form a hinge so that the frame can be opened to insert and remove pictures. One large frame is enough, but smaller ones can be made for smaller pictures.

It is a good idea for the specialist to keep on hand a supply of tools for making quick repairs and adjustments of the equipment he uses. This could include a pair of scissors, a screwdriver, pliers, a small hammer, tape, string, glue, and perhaps a small knife or a razor blade. These must be stored where children can never get at them.

Rhythm instruments and other apparatus for specific activities are listed in chapters to follow with discussions of their use and purpose.

An ideal music room with ideal equipment is hard to find, but a very satisfactory program can be worked out even when some of the things described have to be omitted. Before cutting anything out of the music plans, however, all possible corrections to the room and all possible additions of equipment should be made. Since each room differs from others in shape, size, furnishings, and location of windows and doors, each teacher will have to decide for himself just how to make his room most serviceable.

Chapter 3

# THE TEACHING TEAM

THE finest educational program in the world would be worth little without competent personnel to carry it out. Teachers and musicians who have completed the required college courses and graduated with degrees in special education or in music are often unequipped to work with retarded children. Apparently, something necessary to the making of a good teacher is missing in these people. In this chapter, we shall consider some of the skills and qualities especially needed by people who work with retarded children.

In addition to their academic backgrounds, teachers need the learning that comes from experience. During their student days, they can get some valuable experience with retarded children by working with them in a school, institution, or camp as a volunteer or as an employee. Residential schools and camps give the worker opportunities to see children in every phase of daily life. The person who has worked with children as they get up in the morning, dress, eat, play, attend classes, bathe, and go to bed has a truer picture of them than one who has only seen them sitting in school. Nonroutine happenings are especially useful for students to observe and deal with since many unexpected things can take place in the course of a school day, and the teacher must be able to cope with each quickly and effectively. Looking after sick children, dealing with tantrums, taking care of an injured child while simultaneously supervising a group, and other such experiences will prove helpful when the new teacher faces similar conditions in his own classroom.

Competency-Based Teacher Education, a teacher-training program that emphasizes the involvement of teacher trainees in authentic teaching situations rather than in lecture and demonstration courses, may give education majors some of the prior experience they need. Students enrolled in CBTE programs are expected to exhibit competency in teaching as part of their requirements for graduation. Perhaps CBTE trainees who lack the necessary qualifications for becoming good teachers will realize it and get out of education before they waste years of study in the wrong discipline

14

and go on to enlarge the already swollen corps of bad teachers.

Whatever their educational backgrounds may be, teachers who are capable of learning will learn more from having the full responsibility of teaching a class than from any other experience, the reason being that a good teacher constantly studies his pupils in order to learn how to teach them. Everything a child says and does, especially the mistakes he makes, are of significance to a teacher who wants to learn how to teach. When a teacher no longer needs to learn, it is time for him to retire. All children are different, and no teacher knows everything about every child.

The teacher should be a person who likes and enjoys retarded children. His job is to help them resolve, counteract, or work around their problems. To do this effectively, the teacher will have to make sure that he relates to the children and not to their problems.

Relating to problems instead of to children may result in attitudes that can hamper the children's development. Pity may show itself in overindulgence and lack of firmness in dealing with the children. Extreme professionalism can make the teacher seem cold and clinical. Overconcern about the children's feelings may cause adults to behave unnaturally — speaking in falsetto, always hiding anger or amusement.

This is not to say that the teacher should be unsympathetic, unprofessional, or unconcerned. The teacher who relates to his pupils as individual human beings will be able to relax and enjoy them. Retarded children are people. The teacher who wants to help them will think of them as people. While keeping the children's problems, goals, and needs in mind, the teacher should react to each child in the way that a warm, considerate person reacts to any "normal" person. Although a teacher needs to maintain a calm, easy, comfortable demeanor, he should not expect to meet every circumstance with an imperturbable exterior. Retarded children live in a world of human beings, and they need teachers who are human beings, not superhuman beings. Therefore, a teacher who has a human-to-human relationship with the children is not afraid of being amused, irritated, sympathetic, or firm. The class, in turn, will be happier and more responsive because they have a warm, human relationship with their teacher.

One of the most important abilities needed by teachers of the retarded is the ability to think creatively. Because retardation exists in varying degrees and because it can be complicated by physical, emotional, or environmental problems (also in varying degrees and in different combinations), each child presents a completely individual set of traits that may require individualized techniques in teaching. The teacher must diagnose each difficulty encountered and then, calling upon knowledge, experience, and ingenuity, discover a way to dissolve that difficulty. This can mean that songs will have to be composed, materials designed, and new activities invented for specific purposes.

Along with creative thinking, a good teacher should have a constant desire to learn more about teaching, about retardation, and about individual pupils. Reading the latest books and articles concerning the education of mentally deficient people can add to the teacher's general background or give him specific ideas about specific problems. Talking with other people who work with the same children can bring forth some very helpful information. A veteran teacher can still learn from other teachers or from aides. Even questions from someone who knows nothing about the subject can sometimes start the creative teacher on a new trend of thought that leads to something very useful.

In reading or in listening to ideas, it is necessary for the teacher to maintain a balanced attitude so that he does not gullibly swallow things whole or stubbornly reject anything new. The teacher has to evaluate each new idea according to how practical and how beneficial it would be when applied to his own class.

People who work with the mentally retarded should not be easily discouraged but must be willing to keep trying different ideas until they find one that succeeds. Even the quickest mind cannot toss out clever device after clever device without failure. Teachers may at times plan and create for days or weeks, only to see the results of such effort flop miserably. Ideas that flop should not be totally discarded as they may prove to be just the right thing some time in the future or they may be what some other child or group needs right now. Each device should be given a fair trial before being thrown out because a slight adjustment or alteration may be all that is needed to make it work.

The teacher of retarded children must learn to look for and to be pleased with small gains over a long period of time. When we remember to expect retarded progress, we are less likely to exert undue pressure on our pupils. It is important, however, to make sure that the children's slow advancement is a result of their retardation and not an indication that the material being taught is too difficult. Teachers will be happier when they learn to join their students in experiencing satisfaction from observing steady progress through small increments of learning. When the steps up the learning ladder are too far apart, teachers and pupils are exhausted by the long, painful struggle, and the realization that another such struggle lies ahead of each success is enough to discourage everyone concerned.

A very helpful skill for the teacher is the ability to avoid problems by anticipating them. This is fairly simple when we are dealing with concrete situations. For example, children who are learning colors sometimes develop strong preferences and want everything to be in their favorite colors. If we know that this is true of some members of a class, we can avoid problems by arranging to use rhythm sticks of only one color when that class plays instruments. When Jimmy, who likes red, sees that all the sticks are green, he will probably take a pair of green sticks without objection; almost every child would rather have green sticks than no sticks when everyone else has green sticks. By using sticks of only one color, we can avoid the problem of having Jimmy angry because Mary has the red sticks he wants or of Barbara sitting with folded arms and refusing to participate because there is only one yellow stick left.

Anticipating problems in teaching is a little more difficult, and perhaps this is why the first example that comes to mind is one in which we failed to foresee possible confusion. For a circus unit, we had several songs about lions. One of these songs was about lions roaring in their cages, and another was about lions rolling on the floor. We did not realize until we began teaching the songs that the words *roar* and *roll* were confusing some of the singers. We corrected that mistake by changing "Hear them roar" to "Hear them growl." Had we anticipated this problem, we would not have confused the children.

One of the most difficult things a teacher has to learn is to limit his vocabulary to the level of the children's understanding. Few people realize how many words they normally use until they try verbal communication with someone who understands only twenty or thirty words. Besides talking simply, it is necessary to speak slowly and clearly and give the child time to absorb the meaning of the question or statement and formulate a reply. Too often, we repeat a question or remark, or even rephrase it, before the child has had a chance to reply.

It is also important to make sure that the children are listening to us when we talk to them. Teachers involved in teaching sometimes forget to notice whether anyone is paying attention. If children are not listening to us, we ought to figure out why. Is the lesson too hard? Are we using too many words? Are the children tired? Is the room too warm? Would doing a few motor activities revitalize the group?

There are times when boys and girls turn off their ears in order to shut out our voices. In our eagerness to reach children and make them understand, we often talk too much, and the poor children suffer from aural fatigue. A good teacher is aware of this danger and tries to avoid dinning into the children's ears.

While teachers may have difficulty expressing themselves clearly to their students, they may find it even more difficult, and at times impossible to understand the speech of some of their pupils. A child may be discouraged from trying to talk if the teacher looks at him blankly or keeps asking, "What?" every time he speaks. The teacher, therefore, will have to learn to listen for clues that may identify the subject of the conversation if nothing else. Since it is easier to understand a child's poor speech when we know what he is talking about and since the child probably talks about the things that interest him, it is helpful to know something of his interests. What do a child's parents do? What are his brothers' and sisters' names? What does he like to do at home? Has anything of special interest taken place in his family recently?

When the teacher knows such things, he is better able to catch a key word that may provide the necessary clue to what the child is saying. If the teacher can make out only the word *Don* in a long string of unidentifiable words spoken by Thelma, knowing that Don is Thelma's brother may help him figure out a few more words that reveal Thelma's thought. Even if he cannot figure out any more words, the teacher can at least respond by saying, "What did Don do?" or "Don is your brother, isn't he?"

If the teacher hears a word but cannot guess what is being said about it, a mere repetition of the word is sometimes enough to satisfy a child or encourage him to continue conversing. Pat says something about a ball. The teacher asks, "Ball?" and Pat nods. This may end the conversation, or Pat may say something further. Knowing that the child is talking about a ball may help the teacher to understand what she says next.

For those times when we are unable to latch on to a key word, a noncommital "Oh?" can be very useful. While it is not always appropriate, it is usually safer than saying, "You did!" or "How nice!"

### THE CLASSROOM TEACHER

Of the people who see a group of children, it is the teacher who has the best opportunities for getting to know each member of the group personally. Others, including the music specialist, see the children for a few minutes a day while the teacher works with them for as much as five or six hours a day. The teacher also has but one small group with which to get acquainted while the specialist must learn to know many children. Obviously then, the teacher is the person who can make the best use of music with his particular group.

This is especially true when the class is made up of very young children. These children have such short attention spans that a music specialist cannot be expected to keep them interested for a fifteen- or twenty-minute period. It is much better for them to stay in their room with their teacher and to have music mixed in with everything they do. If the teacher wants to have a music period, he should keep it very short — perhaps five minutes for body rhythms or for playing instruments. Much of the singing can be done in conjunction with the scheduled classroom activities, group or individual, because the songs will make better sense for the children when they can see exactly what they are singing about. Obviously, the music specialist cannot run this type of program because he would have to be in one classroom all day long.

We are presupposing the existence of a well-planned and well-executed educational program that works without music. Our suggestion is that the classroom teacher use music wherever it fits into the daily schedule to make the basic educational program work better. Even when unscheduled, music can be used to relax tension or to perk up a tired group. It is convenient to have a few recordings, songs, finger plays, or simple dances ready to introduce at odd moments during the day either for a specific purpose or merely as a time filler.

## THE MUSIC SPECIALIST

While it is not possible for anyone to have too much formal musical training, it is possible for a serious musician who looks for perfection in his art to be unhappy and ineffectual with children whose efforts are almost always short of perfection. The music specialist needs to think of himself as a teacher rather than as a musician. Otherwise, he would do better to remain in strictly musical circles where he will be forgiven if he throws a tantrum when someone flats or forgets to blow a horn.

A music teacher is a person who teaches people to make music. For him, music is the end product. The music specialist in a school for the retarded is interested in using music as a means to help children reach the goals set by the school program, and he is not particularly concerned with music as a goal in itself. This means that he may at times have to sacrifice artistry for the sake of practicality. He must be willing to play music more slowly than he wants to play it, in order to accommodate the speech or body tempos of the children; he should exaggerate accents and phrasing when doing so will make things clearer for his pupils; and he must resist the urge to use music that is more interesting to him but less useful for teaching purposes.

The music specialist's work also differs from that of the music therapist in that its primary purpose is *teaching*, not *therapy*.

Because the music program must enhance the classroom program, the specialist needs to know as much about retarded children as any good teacher knows. Some knowledge of this kind can be found in books and courses in education, but most of the proficiency in dealing with problems in teaching comes through experience in detecting, analyzing, and solving problems as they arise. It is therefore profitable—even necessary—for the music specialist to have a few years of experience as a classroom teacher of retarded children. His skill in the use of music should be in addition to his skill in teaching.

Besides being familiar with general classroom aims and procedures, the specialist also needs to know the medical, psychological, educational, and family histories of each student. In addition, he should have up-to-date information about the children's development and progress or the lack of it. He can get this information through discussions with teachers and other staff personnel and by studying student records and goals. However, he should not place total reliance on the reports he hears or reads but must maintain a wait-and-see attitude toward the children and their capabilities.

Let us say, for example, that a teacher's report states that Lyndon no longer has temper tantrums. If the music specialist accepts this statement, he may feel unnerved and disheartened when Lyndon puts on a first-rate kicking and screaming demonstration ten minutes after he enters the music room on the first day of school. What the specialist needs to do is to realize that he is dealing with a child who has stopped having tantrums but who, in a new situation with a new teacher, could revert to his former behavior. Thus prepared, the specialist would be better able to handle Lyndon's display of fury.

The specialist may also find conflicting and/or mistaken opinions in the school records. Michael's teacher objected to his being an acrobat doing somersaults in a program because the child could not do somersaults. The music specialist could not believe her ears; whenever she suggested that Michael turn somersaults, he performed one right after another until he reached the other side of the room, then turned around and somersaulted all the way back. Three weeks later, at the rehearsal for the program, Michael still ignored the teacher when she told him it was time to do his somersaults; so to make sure that the boy would do his part at the performance for parents, the teacher asked the music specialist to tell Michael when to do his act.

A new teacher or specialist, upon hearing or reading two different reports of Michael's ability to turn somersaults, would have to find out the truth for himself. The specialist who has to learn about many children will find the school records to be helpful, but he must remember to view the information in the light of his own observations and experience.

The music specialist can make himself most useful by concentrating on those activities the teacher feels least capable of conducting. If the teacher is able to teach songs, for example, the specialist can spend less time on songs and give more attention to something the teacher is unable to do—teach rhythm instruments, perhaps.

The teacher may also need help in the selection of songs or recordings, and the music specialist can take the responsibility for finding or composing suitable material for the teacher to use. The specialist's concern must be to support the teacher's efforts to help the children and not to set up his own program with his own personal goals in view.

Because the music period is a rather informal time, the specialist will have to be careful to keep it from getting wild. In order to sustain the feeling of pleasure and release imparted by the music, the children must be allowed a degree of freedom, but that freedom needs to be contained within a definite framework of class procedure and limits. The specialist must keep things under control and yet not stifle the children's spontaneity. Perhaps a few examples will give the reader an idea of how to achieve order without imposing rigid controls on the children.

The children are taking turns running to music. When the song has been played once, the runner is to sit down and let someone else have a turn. But Cindy does not sit when her turn is over. The music specialist, seeing that the girl needs to work off more energy, plays the song another time, or perhaps even two more times. Now, Cindy is ready to sit down. What if the adult simply demands that the child sit right away? Cindy may sit, but she may fidget or get up again because she still needs to be in motion.

On days when most or all of the children are acting like Cindy, the teacher can just forget about turns and let everybody do things together. And what about the carefully thought out plans for the day? Forcing them on the group will accomplish nothing anyway; so why not just give them what they need? It will not be time wasted.

Gary is a tease. Whenever another child stands up, Gary runs to sit in that child's chair. But when a child or the teacher asks him to return to his own place, he quickly complies. Douglas is different. He refuses to go back to his own chair. The more his victim screams and cries, the happier he is. The teacher could pull him or carry him back to his chair, but instead, she asks Douglas to help pass out instruments to the class. When Douglas rises to do so, the other child slips back into his chair.

Becky is angry because Jerry entered the room before she did. She is letting her displeasure be known by refusing to sit with the rest of the class. She picks up a chair and carries it to the far end of the room and sits with her back to everyone. The teacher calls her, but she does not answer. Soon, Becky realizes that something is going on, and she turns around to look. The teacher is passing out drums! Becky likes to play the drums. Now, the music starts, and the drums begin to boom. Becky hurriedly drags her chair back and joins the others.

Karen is an unhappy child. Life at home is extremely unpleasant. Any little thing can start the girl crying and slapping herself. Fortunately, she is easy to humor. A word of sympathy or an arm around her shoulder would only increase her bawling, but she can be brought around through her appreciation of the comic and her pride in being able to pronounce the teacher's name. Gary has taken Karen's chair. Karen stamps her foot, screams, folds her arms, scowls, and sticks out her lower lip. The teacher goes to Karen, gets down to her level, folds her arms, scowls, and sticks out her lower lip. Karen cannot help smiling when she sees the teacher's funny face.

"What's my name?" asks the teacher.

"Hoshizaki!"

"Right!"

Karen laughs. The teacher takes her over to Gary and says, "Tell Gary to move."

"Move!" demands Karen.

And Gary moves.

Today, the children have come in shouting and complaining. Guy hit Peter, and Peter hit Karl, and now everyone is hitting everyone else. There is no point in telling the class that they should not hit each other or in asking them to sing, for they will continue to hit—and not even in rhythm. So, if they want to hit, we will give them tambourines and cymbals and let them march around hitting the instruments as hard as they like.

As a gross motor exercise, the children are jumping to music. Suddenly, one child accidentally bumps another and decides it would be fun to purposely bump everyone. Soon, half the group is bumping instead of jumping. The teacher goes to the cupboard and gets a long block for each child and demonstrates how to jump over the block. The children become so interested in jumping over their blocks that they forget to bump.

Paul loves music and does not want to leave. When the next class enters and is ready to begin, Paul is still sitting there saying, "No." The teacher has an idea. She opens the door to the hall, starts playing the piano, and says, "March." Paul jumps to his feet and marches out of the room and down the hall to his next class.

Mark and John are good friends and like to sit next to each other. Their friendship is disturbing to the class, however, as they fool around and make sounds like grunting pigs. The teacher has the group play a game in which one child walks, runs, or skips around the room and then points to another child who takes his turn while the first child takes the vacated chair. When the game is over, Mark and John are no longer sitting next to each other.

Joey, whose severe emotional problems had caused him to be functionally retarded, is beginning to show his actual superior mentality but he is still extremely aggressive and difficult to work with. The music specialist is new in the school, and Joey is daring her to try to control him. He dashes into the room with a yell, tears around for a while, drags a chair to the middle of the room, stands on it with one arm raised high, and shouts, "I am the Statue of Liberty!" The specialist has heard that Joey is very much interested in numbers, so she gets an electronic metronome that has a synchronized flashing light, starts it, and places it where it can easily be seen.

The "Statue of Liberty" is now screaming and racing about, recruiting others to join him. On one of his trips to the end of the room where the teacher is sitting, he sees the metronome light flashing and stops to inspect it. When he asks, "What is that?" the teacher gives him a brief explanation of what the instrument does and shows him how to set it at lower or higher numbers to make it tick and flash at lower or higher speeds. Joey sets it at various positions on the dial and is pleased to see what it does. The teacher now sits at the piano and begins to play in time with the metronome, and Joey marches around with the music. When the march is over, he returns to the metronome and sets it at a different tempo. The teacher plays something to fit the new tempo, and Joey and all the other children move to the music. Soon the class is having a very pleasant rhythm session; the teacher has taken over, and Joey has become just another member of the group. There will be other difficult days, but the worst is over because Joey has found that the teacher is neither intimidated nor angered by his behavior and that she has something interesting to offer.

These examples serve to illustrate how order can be maintained in the music room by giving a child the opportunity to change his behavior without being forced to do so. In each instance, it was necessary for the adult in charge to know the children well. Cindy could be given an extra turn because the teacher knew that she would sit down when she had run around enough. Dan, another child in the same group, would not have been given a second turn because he habitually did the opposite of what adults wanted him to do. The teacher would therefore have taken him back to his chair when his turn was over.

The teacher would not have had Douglas pass out instruments in order to get him out of someone else's chair if Douglas or others in the class considered passing out instruments a special privilege. Similarly, she would not have made a face for Karen if she had not known that Karen would be amused by it.

Again, the teacher would not have opened the door and played the piano so that Paul could march out of the room if members of the next class were likely to go marching out with Paul.

We hope the reader does not conclude that the primary concern of the music specialist is peace at any price, for children will never learn to adjust to situations if we always adjust situations to them. But there are reasons for the specialist to avoid any serious unpleasantness with the classes. The specialist sees the children for only a few minutes each day, and if he is unable to resolve difficulties before the group leaves, the classroom teacher must then handle the situation. This is bad for all—child, specialist, and teacher. Also, since the music period is short, it is unfortunate to have to use large chunks of time demanding compliance from the children.

It takes skill to keep the children's freedom, control, and self-expression in balance, and it is a skill worth developing as it reduces the need for disciplinary action. This brings about happier relationships between the music specialist and the children.

We have tried to describe some of the duties of a music specialist and to draw an image of the kind of person he needs to be. If these are not to the liking of the musician we suggest that he investigate further and think carefully before committing himself to specializing in music with retarded children.

## THE ASSISTANT

In work with retarded children, particularly those with multiple handicaps or social and emotional problems, there is nothing to be treasured more highly than a good assistant. When a teacher works alone, his attention has to be scattered, and he often has to do a good deal of moving around. If he is working with one child, for instance, he must also keep track of what everyone else is doing and take care of unscheduled events such as accidents, fights, toileting problems, and destruction of property. With an assistant to take over some of these responsibilities, the teacher can concentrate more fully on actual teaching.

The assistant must first know and understand what the teacher is trying to do; after that, everything he does should be aimed at helping the teacher achieve his purpose with the group. No matter how kind and helpful an assistant tries to be, he is a distraction and a hindrance if he cannot take the teacher's goals as his own.

The teacher will need to tell the assistant about each child. He may have to give rather explicit instructions on what to do about some of the more difficult children. It will usually be a help to the teacher if the aide works with children who have the most trouble paying attention or staying with the group.

When the teacher is directing the entire class, the assistant should not talk any more than necessary, either to the children or to the teacher. He must be alert and ready to help and be able to refrain from helping children who can do things without help. In order not to confuse the children, a good assistant will follow the teacher's lead when something out of the ordinary happens, even if he does not know or understand the reasons for the teacher's actions.

An assistant should feel free to ask questions when having consultations with the teacher. And the teacher would be wise to give serious consideration to the suggestions of a good assistant.

A music specialist may find that the classroom teacher makes a good aide because he knows the children. The children may also respond better to their teacher than they would to anyone else. On the other hand, the classroom teacher can prove to be the worst possible helper if his philosophies and methods differ greatly from those of the specialist or if he insists upon running the class. Of course, in the case of a poor teacher, the farther he stays from the music room, the better it will be for everyone.

There is another problem that sometimes arises when the teacher is present during music sessions. A few children, seeing that their teacher is not as busy as usual, decide that this is the time to claim his attention. These children insist upon sitting next to the teacher and refuse to do anything unless he does it with them, even though they can get along beautifully when he is not there.

The teacher's manner should always show respect and appreciation for his assistant. However, the assistant must not be disturbed if the teacher sounds abrupt at times because, when things are hectic and there is no time for explanations, the teacher may have to make requests very concisely. Music specialists will find that a good assistant makes the work go more smoothly and that sharing observations and ideas with an aide can result in an improved program.

Chapter 4

# WHERE TO START

BEFORE setting up a music program, it is necessary to determine each child's musical ability and his level of achievement in other areas of his life. Evaluating the musical abilities of our students gives us the information we need in order to decide what musical techniques will be most effective in working with our groups.

The simplest way to record our findings is to put them on charts. The charts put the needed information in concise and easy-to-read form, but when a child is moved from one class to another, it becomes necessary to cross out all the data on him from one chart and transfer it to another. At the beginning of a school year, the children may be regrouped; then all the marks have to be copied onto new charts. To cut out all this extra work, we suggest the following method of charting.

We shall need a presentation binder (a loose leaf folder of the kind used by salesmen to present a catalog of their wares). If we have a binder that takes 8½" × 11" sheets, we can use one with twenty-two rings and paper with twenty-two holes (larger binders are also available). An easel type binder is good because it can stand on top of the piano or other convenient place.

On a sheet of 8½" × 11" paper, make a chart similar to the one shown in Figure 1. Make photocopies of the chart on 22-hole paper. The holes should be at the top of the chart. (If you punch your own paper, make the holes no more than 3/16" in diameter. 1/8" holes are even better, provided the rings are not too big for them). Now cut the individual lists apart so that there is a 2" × 8½" strip for each child in the class.

Before placing the strips inside the folder, insert a sheet of strong, heavy paper (a notebook divider is fine). Starting at the right, put one strip into the binder. Place the second list to the left, overlapping the first, but leaving the checking space uncovered. The third is placed to the left of the second, and the process is continued until we have a list for each member of the class. The fewer in the class, of

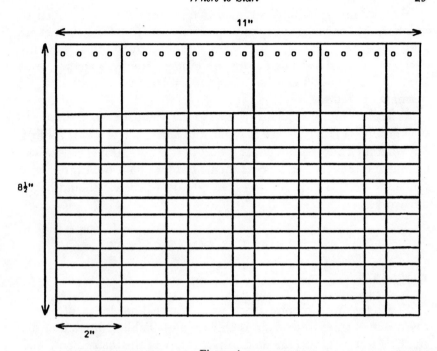

Figure 1.

course, the less overlapping will have to be done. If there are more than ten people in a class, another page will be needed. (This is the way our charts were made, but the reader may find that using different dimensions or materials will suit his or her needs more efficiently.)

There are acetate sheet protectors into which the chart, with its heavy paper support, can be placed. This makes page-flipping easier and keeps the charts from being torn or decorated by children. If used just as it comes, the sheet protector cannot be opened unless the front of it is lifted off the rings. To make it simpler to open the protector when we want to make new entries on the lists, we can cut a strip lengthwise off the front of it, right through the holes. It will still slip under the narrow flap that keeps the folder closed, but it can be pulled out without opening the rings and placed under the heavy sheet that supports the lists while we write on the chart.

All the charts can be prepared in the same way, and those for each class can be separated from the others by tabbed dividers.

This is a great deal of work, but once it is done, it will not have to be done again. If a child is removed from one class and placed in another, it is only necessary to remove his lists from one class chart and place them in another. When a child leaves the school, his checklists can be removed from the binder, stapled together, and kept, or information can be taken from them and written into his permanent record.

When the music specialist is new to the school or when there are new groups of children, we may have to spend a few weeks finding out what the children can do. It is best to start at a simple level when testing and make upward adjustments until we have discovered how much the groups have already learned and where we should begin our work.

## MUSICAL GOALS

### Instruments

Plans for instrumental work will require knowledge of which rhythm instruments the child is able to play. Table I shows that the children in this group are able to play most of the instruments and that they are beginning to play some of them in time to the music. All of these children will have opportunities to play the various instruments, but for a rhythm band, we will assign instruments according to the children's abilities.

Hand preference is recorded because children's difficulties with an instrument are sometimes caused by trying to play with the wrong hand. There will be times, however, when we shall want to give children practice in using the hand with which they are less skillful.

Table II shows that only one child in the group is not able to start playing when the music starts and stop playing when the music stops. Two of the five can start and stop on spoken command, no matter what the music does. And only Amy is able to follow a visual cue. For this group, we should probably say, "Go," when the music starts, and "Stop," when the music stops, to help Dean get the idea. The three who cannot follow spoken signals will probably be given individual chances to wait for "Go" before starting to play, and playing until they hear "Stop." For Ken's sake, the director can combine a nod of the head with "Go," and a shake of the head with "Stop,"

Table - I

| INSTRUMENTS | | | | | |
|---|---|---|---|---|---|
| | Steven | Nancy | Susan | John | Stacey |
| Sleighbells | √ | √ | √ | √ | √ |
| Rattle | √ | √ | √ | √ | √ |
| Drum | T | T | T | √ | √ |
| Sticks | T | √ | T | √ | √ |
| Jingle clog | √ | √ | √ | √ | √ |
| Sandblocks | √ | √ | √ | √ | √ |
| Cymbals | √ | √ | √ | √ | √ |
| Tambourine<br>Hit \| Shake | T \| √ | √ \| O | √ \| √ | √ \| O | √ \| √ |
| Horn | √ | √ | √ | √ | √ |
| Triangle | √ | √ | √ | √ | √ |
| Castanets | √ | O | √ | O | O |
| Finger cymbals | √ | O | √ | O | O |

√ = can play
T = can play in time to music
O = cannot play
Date = when first able to play

Table II

| RESPONSE TO SIGNALS | | | | | |
|---|---|---|---|---|---|
| | David | Dean | Claude | Amy | Ken |
| Start, stop with music | √ | O | √ | √ | √ |
| Start, stop on spoken command | O | O | O | √ | √ |
| Start, stop on visual cue | O | O | O | April 1979 | O |

O = cannot do
√ = can do
Date = when first able to do

so that he will learn to associate the words with the gestures.

### Tempo and Volume

Some children do not make a visible or audible response to changes in tempo; if the music gets faster or slower, they do not move or sing faster or slower. Table III indicates that the children of this group are not very much aware of tempo differences.

**Table III**

| RESPONSE TO CHANGES | | | | | |
|---|---|---|---|---|---|
| | Mark | Michael | Barry | Charles | Joseph |
| In tempo | NR | NR | App. | NR | April 1979 |
| In volume | R | App. | April 1979 | R | App. |

NR  = no response
R  = makes response
App.  = makes appropriate response
Date  = when first able to give appropriate response

Changes in volume are easier to detect. The table shows that three boys respond to changes in volume but that they do not respond appropriately; when they hear music get louder, they respond by laughing or by playing faster, not by playing louder.

The specialist could not expect this group to play rhythm band music that requires them to play softly or loudly in different parts or music that makes sudden changes in tempo. However, he can use songs and instrumental and motor activities in ways that will help these children listen attentively for differences in speed and volume.

### Gross Motor Skills

Handedness and footedness are placed at the top of Table IV because they can sometimes make a difference in the performance of gross motor activities. This table tells which movements the children can make and whether or not they can do them in time to the music.

**Table IV**

| GROSS MOTOR SKILLS | | | | | |
|---|---|---|---|---|---|
| | Joan | Beryl | Jim | Ron | Scott |
| Preferred hand | right | left | left | right | right |
| Preferred foot | ? | ? | left | right | right |
| Clap | √ | √ | √ | √ | √ |
| Walk | √ | √ | √ | T | √ |
| Run | √ | √ | √ | T | √ |
| Sway | √ | O | √ | √ | √ |
| Tiptoe | √ | O | Nov. 1977 | T | √ |
| Jump | √ | O | Jan. 1979 | √ | √ |
| Gallop | April 1979 | March 1980 | O | √ | May 1979 |
| Slide<br>Left \| Right | O \| O | O \| O | O \| O | O \| √ | O \| O |
| Hop<br>Left \| Right | O \| O | O \| O | O \| O | O \| √ | O \| Apr. 1979 |
| Skip | O | O | O | O | O |

√ = can do
T = can do in time to music
O = cannot do
Date = when first able to do

Many children learn to recognize music they have heard over and over again, and they remember what movements they make to that music. Some of them immediately react appropriately to music they have never heard before. Others gradually learn to hear differences in the music. Table V shows which children can recognize typical rhythms in unfamiliar music. Jumping and running music apparently are easiest to identify.

Table V

| TYPICAL RHYTHMS | | | | | |
| --- | --- | --- | --- | --- | --- |
| | Claude | Amy | Marlene | Kathy | Ken |
| Walk | O | √ | O | O | O |
| Run | O | √ | √ | √ | O |
| Sway | O | √ | O | O | O |
| Tiptoe | O | √ | O | O | O |
| Jump | √ | √ | √ | O | O |
| Skip or Gallop | O | √ | O | O | O |

√ = can tell or make appropriate motion
Date = when first able to recognize the rhythm
O = cannot give appropriate response

Some of the music used for body rhythm exercises can be familiar, but new music should be introduced from time to time so that the children will listen attentively and become aware of the character of the music instead of automatically reacting to the tunes they are used to hearing.

## CLASSROOM GOALS

When the musical abilities of the pupils have been determined and we have some idea of the methods to use with the various groups, it is important to know the goals toward which the musical methods will be applied. The music specialist should therefore study the classroom records of each child's accomplishments and goals before planning the music program.

We have to say here, though we dislike doing it, that the music specialist needs to make sure that the information contained in the records is correct and that the goals are logical and realistic. We do not suggest that the music specialist test the children and challenge the teacher whose observations differ from his own. This would be neither feasible nor wise. It is important, however, for the specialist to have accurate assessments of the students' abilities in order to prepare activities and materials that will reinforce the skills already attained and will be of value in the acquisition of new ones. If the specialist bases his work on inaccurate evaluations, his efforts will be wasted at best and harmful at worst. As soon as he realizes that his work is missing the point, the specialist should stop that particular activity. Three examples are given here to show what can happen when lessons are based on mistaken views of the children's accomplishments.

Ms. Long proudly announced at a teachers' meeting that all the children in her class had learned the numbers from one through ten. They understood the concept of numbers and could also read and write the numerals from one through ten. In fact, the kids had been drilled so thoroughly and had learned the lesson so well that they were sick and tired of one through ten and were ready to go on to bigger and better things.

This class was to be prepared for future workshop experience. The music specialist was delighted that she could now try out some new ideas with the group. At that time, people in the workshop had a job that consisted of putting specified numbers of objects into small plastic bags. The specialist therefore planned an activity that would give the class practice in counting and withdrawing a certain number of rhythm sticks from a box.

The group sat at one side of a long table. A box of rhythm sticks was placed in front of the boy at one end of the table. As everyone sang, "Take one stick and pass the box," the first boy was to take one stick and slide the box to his neighbor, and the process was to be repeated down the line until everyone had had a turn.

Everything went perfectly. Now, they would sing, "Take two sticks and pass the box," and proceed as before. Some children took two sticks. Others took only one. The specialist showed them how to take two sticks. Some took two, and some took one. The specialist explained that they were to take *two* sticks — *one, two*. Some took two, Alice took three, Leonard took a handful, Keith took one.

At this point, the music specialist gave up the lesson and used the rest of the period to find out more about these children and their conception of numbers. By having them help her ready the room for the next music group, she found that only a few understood numbers. Keith always brought one of any item, no matter how many he was asked to bring. Alice and Leonard brought as many as they happened to pick up. The few who were able to successfully respond to requests for a certain number of things could do so only up to three. If they were asked to get four rattles or five bells, they were unable to do it.

In another case, the music specialist decided to have a group play games in which they could use the colors they knew and perhaps get some practice in recognizing the colors they were learning. She found that the teacher had set down many colors for each child to learn. Clare's immediate goal, for example, was to learn "orange, red, green, blue, purple, brown, and black." Realizing that a retarded child confronted with that many colors to learn at once would be overwhelmed the specialist gave up the idea of musical color games for the group.

In yet another instance, the music specialist was informed by the teacher that John was able to read his name. The specialist found, however, that John thought that *John, Joan, Joke,* and *Jean* all spelled *John.* Thinking that the boy could not see the difference between words of the same length and similar contours, the specialist tried *Jello, Jump, Juice.* John thought each was his name. Finally, the specialist showed him longer words: *Joseph, Jupiter, Jealous.* He thought they all spelled *John.*

John was the only one in his class whose name began with *J.* Apparently, his teacher had never included other words beginning with *J* in the list from which John was to choose his name. Since he obviously had learned to recognize the letter *J,* John was ready to learn that all words beginning with *J* are not the same. He did not yet know his name when he saw it.

In each of these examples, the music specialist dropped the lessons because they were not appropriate for the groups or individuals for whom they had been prepared. She did not revise her plans and make up new activities commensurate with the children's abilities in each case. The reason for this was that she did not feel it necessary to work against the convictions of the classroom teacher, because it was possible to have a well-rounded music program even without that particular activity.

In a school where there are no well-defined goals and where nothing is done systematically, a specialist must set up his music program on the basis of his own observations of the children. It may be that in this situation, most of the music activities should be concentrated on motor skills and the playing of instruments since it is easier to see ability levels in these areas than in others.

Chapter 5

# SONGS

THIS chapter is concerned with songs that are used for teaching purposes and not with songs sung just for fun. Although popular music such as that heard on radio and television is not discussed here, the reader is not to conclude that popular music must be avoided. It is important for retarded children to experience the same kinds of music that other children enjoy. Residential schools must make a special effort to see that their children have opportunities to hear, sing, and dance to the current popular favorites so that they will be ready to fit in with the musical interests of brothers and sisters and friends when they go home. This type of music can be used during recreation periods, or it can be played by children on their own radios and record players when they have free time.

To make music function as effectively as possible in the classroom, it is best to keep the music used for recreational purposes separate from the music used for teaching. It is hard for children to attend to a lesson that is presented in music they have frequently heard while relaxing or playing or to which they are used to dancing.

First of all, songs must be chosen for suitable subject matter. They may be about things the children already know, or they may be about things that are being learned. There is little educational value in singing about something totally foreign to one's experiences.

Before we can begin choosing songs, we shall have to know something about each boy and girl in the class. If the songs are to be about something the children know, a good place to start is with the child himself. Songs about one's own person, the things one does, and the things one has—these should be among the easiest subjects for our songs. It is a mistake, however, to assume that all children are most interested in themselves; there are some who do not like themselves, and there are some who do not like their families. Others are not even sure who they are. And some children are more interested in cars or airplanes than in people.

Until the teacher is well informed as to the children's backgrounds, the safest thing to do is to sing about school activities. Since the children and the teacher are in the same physical surroundings and take part in the same routines and experiences from day to day, songs about the things that take place in school should be suitable for all.

As the teacher learns more about the class, he will find more for the children to sing about, and as the children's experiences broaden, the number of song possibilities will grow.

When we have selected a suitable song topic, the next thing we must do is to make sure that what we say about the topic is comprehensible to those who sing. At Thanksgiving time, for example, everyone in the school may be talking about Thanksgiving and the things related to that holiday. But not all things connected with Thanksgiving are understood by all retarded children. To some, the "Pilgrim Fathers" may simply mean "Father." For many, "thanks" may only be the word one says upon receiving a gift, and the idea of being thankful for past blessings or for the everyday things we enjoy may be impossible to grasp.

When a teacher exclaimed, "Thanksgiving is coming!" Colleen asked, "Where?" Colleen had learned that when people *come*, they come to a *place*. But who was Thanksgiving? It probably would not have helped for the teacher to say, "Thanksgiving Day," as Colleen would have thought that Day was a last name. The problem was that the girl did not yet understand the relationship of *today* to *yesterday* and *tomorrow*, and when one does not know that one day is in the present, another in the past, and another in the future, one cannot be expected to understand that there is a special day coming several days or even weeks in the future.

For people like Colleen, then, "Thanksgiving is coming" would not be a good song. "We gather together to ask the Lord's blessing" would be just as inappropriate as songs should come straight from the children's experience. Colleen's class had helped make a pumpkin pie and had eaten it as part of their Thanksgiving experience. Depending upon their language ability, a class like this might sing, "We made a pumpkin pie," "I like pumpkin pie," or "Yum, yum, pumpkin pie."

Children who understand that turkeys are birds that we cook and eat can sing about turkeys that say, "Gobble, gobble," and also about turkeys that we eat. Children who have not learned the connection between the barnyard fowl and the decapitated, plucked, brown

hunk of meat on a platter might be better off singing, "I like turkey and gravy" as a Thanksgiving song, and leaving "The turkey
says, 'Gobble, gobble'" for a time when they are singing about
animals.

Teachers should also be careful to select songs about present-day
objects and activities. Many books still contain songs about things
that are no longer in frequent use. It is no longer appropriate to
show children how to make scrubbing motions while singing, "This
is the way we wash our clothes." Most children have never seen a
washboard, so for them, "We are loading the washing machine" is a
better song.

Electric clocks that do not tick and diesel-powered trains that do
not chug are more examples of song topics that require different
lyrics from the songs of earlier years. Even Christmas has had to be
updated. Many sets of words are sung to "O, Christmas Tree," and
most of them are in praise of the sturdy evergreen. One year, we
decided that our educable groups, who knew their colors well, needed a new stanza to account for all the differently colored trees they
saw. The result, though true, was not beautiful:

> Sometimes the trees are pink or red,
> Or blue or white or gold instead.
> The shiny metal trees aren't real;
> They're aluminum or stainless steel.

A good song employs words the children know. Ellison, in speaking of children in the grades, suggests the meaning of the words as a
valid criterion for choosing songs suitable for various age groups.
Children will not understand the meaning of the words unless they
have had experiences broad enough to cover the significance of the
words (Ellison, 1959). Retarded children with limited language and
limited experiences need songs with a limited vocabulary.

If several classes are learning about the same thing, they may
need different songs because of the differences in knowledge and
ability. At times it may be possible to use the same tune with a different set of lyrics for each group. Once, when groups of young
trainables were learning to care for their goldfish, some older
children were asked to help write a song for them. The song turned
out as follows:

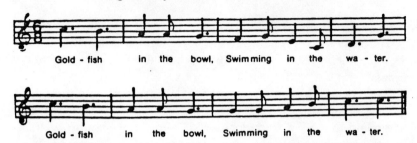

The words were too hard for the little children, and it was necessary to simplify them:

> Goldfish, goldfish,
> Swimming in the water.

And for the youngest group, the words had to be simplified even further:

> Fish, fish, fish, fish,
> Swimming, swimming, swimming.

The joy and enthusiasm with which a child sings a song is not a reliable indication of its suitability. Children with good speech and low language comprehension may be able to sing anything they are taught and yet have no idea of what they are singing.

Timmy was six years old and had excellent speech, some language comprehension, and no communicative language other than shrieking. His speech consisted of repetitions of things people said or parts of songs. He learned songs very quickly and sang all the notes and words correctly, though he did not understand the lyrics at all.

To prove that Timmy could sing anything he heard whether he understood it or not, the music specialist sang some Gilbert and Sullivan songs for him, and soon Timmy was singing, "Bow, bow, ye lower middle classes," and "I am the very pattern of a modern major-general." If he had listened to Wagner and Verdi, Timmy would undoubtedly have hopped around his room, singing, "*Dir, Göttin der Liebe soll mein Lied ertönen,*" or "*Si, vendetta, tremenda vendetta.*"

Singing words he did not understand was all right for Timmy's own entertainment, for he loved music and had almost no other interests, but when he was taught anything through music, the words had to be limited to those he could understand.

Simplifying the lyrics will not be enough for children who have not learned to talk at all. For these children, we take a simple song, remove all the words, and substitute a neutral syllable the children can say—*ba, ba; ta, ta; mi, mi*—and we have a syllable song. Be careful not to use *ma, ma* when there is a homesick child in the group.

It is sometimes possible to give meaning even to a syllable song. Show a picture of a dog, for instance, and let the children sing "Arf, arf," or "Woof, woof," to show what a dog says, and the syllable has become a word.

A child who can say only one word of a song that the other children sing may be encouraged to sing that one word throughout the entire song if he wants to do it. Some children who cannot say words can make very realistic sound effects, and they enjoy taking part in songs that give them a chance to supply a lion's roar, the scream of a siren, or the rumbling of a truck.

Another type of one-word song is the verb song. Verb songs are easy to understand because they can be acted out, thus associating word with meaning:

Run, run, run, run,   run, run, run, run.

Gal - lop,   gal - lop,   gal - lop,   gal - lop.

Tip - toe,   tip - toe,   tip - toe,   tip - toe.

The third type of one-word song is the noun song. Noun songs should be related to the objects named in the songs through the use of those objects themselves or their miniature or pictorial representations. The one-word noun song is not very interesting, especially when sung by a group. It can be effective, however, when used by an adult working with one child. For example, a teacher who is helping a child put on his shoe can sing, "Shoe, shoe, shoe." The teacher will have to make sure that the child knows what he is singing about by showing him the shoe or having him hold it. Singing, because of the changes in pitch, may hold a child's attention better than merely saying words.

A song that is used to teach a new word should contain words the children know already, except for that one new word. This calls attention to the new word and eliminates the possibility of confusing the meanings of two or more new words. If the idea being taught is expressed in a combination of words, that combination of words will take the place of a single new word. At Halloween, for example, we may want to sing a song about lighting the candle in a jack-o'-lantern. We would then sing, "Light the candle," even though both *light* and *candle* are new words.

Our songs should use the commonly used names for things. Few people refer to the person who delivers mail as the "postman." Yet when a mailman gets into a song, he often becomes a postman. Even if we think that "postman" sounds better in a song, we should use "mailman" if that is what the children are used to calling him. If some children have a maillady or mailwoman coming to their homes, we shall have to accommodate them by fitting those people into the songs.*

Common usage must also determine the arrangement of words in a song. Making lines rhyme is not as important as making the words sound natural. The children have enough language difficulties without having to cope with lyrics like —

> Happy are we
> When holidays come.
> Sing you with glee,
> And beat now the drum.

For very young retardates or for low grade trainables, a song should have only one or two ideas that are repeated over and over:

> We talk to our friends.
> We talk to our friends.
> We talk to our friends on the bus.
> We talk to our friends.

---

*We question the use of words like "mailperson." We have to work so hard to teach some children to use "woman," "man," "girl," "boy," and their respective pronouns correctly that it is downright depressing to think of teaching about a "mailperson."

We talk to our friends.
But never talk to strangers.

Fortunately, children like repetition and do not tire of the same words or the same songs very easily. (This particular lesson backfired one day when Preston sat down next to a stranger on the bus, poked the man's arm, and said, "Me no talk *you!*" The gesture and facial expression that accompanied the words left no doubt as to how Preston felt about strangers.)

We have been thinking of how to choose or to write words for a song. Now let us consider the music for our songs. The music, especially for very little children, should be very simple. Children naturally use two notes in calling or chanting:

Tom - my

The interval between these two tones is what musicians refer to as a minor third. Because the second tone is lower than the first, the interval is called a descending minor third. The tones are *sol* and *mi* of the scale.

Many teachers and mothers have unwittingly used these two tones when singing to children. For example:

Come, Sus - ie.   Here   we   go.

Kodaly and Orff have used these natural singing tones as a starting point in their music education systems. Children often add another tone, *la*, of the scale, when they chant to or at each other:

I'm going   to   have   a   par - ty.

To these three tones, add *do* and *re*. This gives us *do, re, mi, sol, la*—a five-tone (or pentatonic) scale. Teachers who do not know music can get an idea of how a five-tone scale sounds by using the black keys of a piano. Find a group of three black keys. Starting with the key on the left, proceed to the right playing each black key until you have played five keys (one group of three and one group of two black keys). This is a five-tone scale. It leaves out *fa* and *ti* of the major scale, which we are used to hearing. Many folk songs are built on this scale.

Sheehy suggests that normal children of nursery school age be exposed to many songs with a range of three to five tones, because being able to learn and sing easy songs encourages children to use their singing voices (Sheehy, 1959). Music educators have found that children need time and experience to learn to sing well. Ellison states that control of the singing voice and the ability to reproduce melodies is a developmental process that is not completed in some children until the middle grades (Ellison, 1959). If young normal children need simple melodies, the teacher of retarded children can be sure that his class needs them too.

The five-tone scale answers the requirement of simplicity if we are careful not to use awkward leaps in our tunes. Even teachers who think they cannot sing may be able to manage two or three of the five tones.

A few retarded children, even at an early age, have the ability to sing very difficult songs on pitch, and these children may be given anything they can sing as long as the words are simple enough for them to understand. But in a group situation, we shall have to stay with songs that suit the abilities of all the children.

We stated earlier that simple songs need much repetition in the words. They also need repetition in the melodic line and in the rhythm patterns. The familiar nursery tune below demonstrates repetition in melody and rhythm.

French

It is immediately evident that the first and last lines are exactly alike. This means that when the first line has been learned, the last line has also been learned. A look at the second line shows us that the first two measures are repeated in the last two; so when the first two measures have been learned, the last two have been learned as well.

The rhythmic pattern is simple indeed. It is a two-bar pattern that is repeated throughout the song:

Another thing to keep in mind when choosing a song is that the rhythm, accent, and phrasing of the words and music should coincide. Perhaps this can be made clear by the following example of a very poor song. Accented syllables are capitalized.

GOOD mornING, ma - RY johnSON. HOW are YOU TO - da - AY?

How many people greet each other with, "GOOD mornING?" And what would maRY johnSON's moTHER say if we taught her child to pronounce her name that way?

Would it not be better to have the rhythm, accent, and the end of the phrase go together logically?

Good MORNing, MA - ry JOHNson. HOW are YOU to - DAY?

This is accomplished by writing the words first and then fitting the music to the rhythm of the words. Clapping or tapping out the rhythm of the words we have written will help clarify the rhythmic pattern we shall want to use for the music. For example:

Come, come, come with me. (Tap. Tap. Tap, tap, tap.)

Everybody, come with me. (Tap, tap, tap, tap, tap, tap, tap.)

This can be translated into musical values.

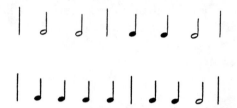

Now, all we need is a simple tune to go with the words and the rhythms.

Come, come,   come with me.    Ev' - ry - bod - y,   come with me.

Often after the children have said the words in rhythm, the teacher can say, "Sing it," to one child, and the child will sing a melody to the words without even thinking about it.

For young children or for the more severely retarded, it is best to limit a song to one stanza. When there are several stanzas, the first is usually the only one that is learned well. Some tunes have more than one set of lyrics, and children who do not understand the words sometimes shift from one set of lyrics to another. Teddy, who had heard many songs at home, treated us to a number of interesting combinations, such as, "Are you sleeping? Are you sleeping? *Dormez vous? Dormez vous?*" and "The bear went over the mountain, For he's a jolly good fellow."

Although Teddy was an educable child with fairly good language skills, he did not really know what he was singing because he did not know French and because his experience did not cover bears and mountains and jolly good fellows. It therefore made no difference to him whether he sang the songs straight or mixed. When children know what the words mean, they are less likely to confuse one set of lyrics with another.

There are occasions, however, when we shall want to have a song that has more than one stanza. One such song can be called a sequence song. This is a song that takes some activity step by step from beginning to end, one stanza for each step in the sequence.

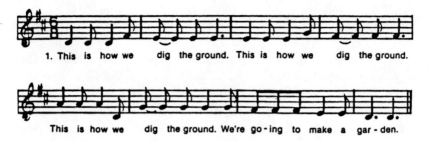

1. This is how we dig the ground. This is how we dig the ground.
This is how we dig the ground. We're go-ing to make a gar-den.

2. This is how we rake the ground.
3. This is how we plant the seeds.
4. This is how we water the seeds.

While teaching a sequence song, it is best to stop after each stanza and talk about the next step in the sequence before continuing with the song. It is also helpful to show an appropriate picture or object to remind the singers what they are to sing about next. Once the sequence is thoroughly learned, the children will be able to sing the song in proper order without help from the teacher. The teacher must have made a good start on the activity before introducing the song, or some children will learn the song by rote, thus defeating the entire purpose of the song.

Akin to the sequence song is the category song. In this kind of song, there is a place into which we can insert any one of several words that belong to the same category. For example, let us take a song about the clothes we wear on a cold day.

It is cold to-day. It is cold to-day. I wore my coat to-day. It is
cold to-day. It is cold to-day. I wore my coat to-day.

The next time through, we might sing *scarf* instead of *coat*. This could be followed by repetitions specifying *gloves, mittens, hat, hood,* or *boots*.

We can similarly treat songs about such categories as food items, playground equipment, motor vehicles, or family members.

Cumulative songs like "Old MacDonald" are easier to sing with cue cards. Pictures of the animals may be placed on a rack as they are added to the song. It is a good idea to place each picture to the left of the preceding one; then when the moos and the oinks and the quacks are sung at the end of each stanza, the animals can be pointed to in order from left to right as in reading. People who find it too hard to go through the entire song in the usual way may sing each stanza as a complete song. When they have chosen an animal to sing about, the singers can place a picture of that animal on the rack. After singing about that animal, they can remove its picture and choose another for the next stanza.

Children can often help make up their own songs. The teacher writes down what they say about some topic. After everyone has said the first line together, the teacher asks one child to sing it. Even if the child sings only a few notes, a complete song can often be constructed from them. The following is a song that was made in this way:

The children had said, "Sweep, sweep the floor." When asked what they needed in order to sweep the floor, they decided that a broom and dustpan were necessary. One of the children was then asked to sing, "Sweep, sweep the floor." He sang the first two measures, and the pattern he set was continued to finish the song.

One morning, Carla happily entered the room saying, "I have a Christmas tree! I have a Christmas tree!" Other children were asked if they also had trees. Michael said, "A big one!" Betty volunteered, "A real one!" And we had a song.

I have a Christmas tree. I have a Christmas tree. A

big one. A real one. I have a Christmas tree.

A song like this is very useful as different words can be substituted in the fourth and fifth measures to make the song personal for each child. "A little one," "A pretty one," or "A green one," are some possibilities. Some children may not understand that each child has his own tree at home, or there may be some who do not have trees. For these children it might be better to sing, "We have a Christmas tree," about the one in the classroom.

At times, it may become necessary to write special words for a child. One day while the class was talking about snow, the teacher noticed that Betty had nothing to say. Even when questioned, the girl smiled and said nothing. The remarks of the others were written down, and the teacher set down the melody as approximated by one child. The result was a song completely understandable to the class.

Snow is nice. Snow is pret - ty. Snow is white. I like snow.

Betty, however, still did not appear interested and would not sing the song. The teacher then asked if she would like to sing about not liking snow. Betty laughed. The teacher asked her, "Is snow nice?"

Betty laughed and answered, "No!"

"Is snow pretty?"

"No! It's messy!"

"Is snow white?"

"Yes."

"Do you like snow?"

"No!" Loud laughter.

The teacher then sang the same tune with revised lyrics.

> Snow is not nice.
> Snow is not pretty.
> Snow is white.
> I don't like snow.

Betty eagerly said, "My turn!" and sang the song by herself with great satisfaction.

This incident clearly illustrates the need for songs that express children's feelings honestly. Betty felt left out because she was the only one of the group who hated snow. She therefore sat quietly instead of joining the discussion and the singing. Another child who disliked snow might have sung the song anyway, but Betty was true to her feelings.

Adults often try to make everything sound wonderful; they forget children are not always happy about things. "Isn't the sunshine beautiful!" (Georgie squints, rubs his eyes, and tries to find some shade.) "What a nice dog!" (David is terrified and refuses to leave the building.) "Sunday is Mother's Day. Be sure to tell your mother that you love her." (Joey hates his mother and wishes her dead.)

It is true that one of the functions of our songs is to create positive feelings toward things that are presently unknown, ignored, misunderstood, disliked, or feared by the children. We may be more successful in doing this, however, if we first let the child know that we understand how he feels and even let him sing his feelings. We should be ready to let children sing gripe songs and hate songs if they need to do so.

It is to be hoped that Betty eventually learned to enjoy throwing snowballs, making snowmen, and sledding, but for the moment, the girl apparently needed to express her disgust with the mess caused by the snow on the streets.

Not all our songs will be composed by the teacher or by the class. There are many song books to be found in book stores, music stores, and libraries, and by systematically going through these books, we may find a few songs that can be used by our children. Sometimes, a very slight alteration in the melody or words is enough to make a song more singable, understandable, or pronounceable. Other songs may require a complete overhaul of words and melody.

Once our songs are composed or selected and altered, we must consider the process for teaching them. The actual teaching will vary with the song and the singers, but we can set down a general plan to follow.

First, begin early. If the songs are about planting in the spring, for example, we need to start a few weeks before planting time. The tune is introduced without mention of what the song is about. For several weeks, the music is used for clapping or for any other suitable body rhythm. When the children are thoroughly familiar with the melody, they may sing it on a neutral syllable.

Now we must wait until planting time has arrived and we have actually prepared the soil and planted the seeds and watered them. After this is done, we can talk about the subject matter of the song, and if we have prepared our song well, the words used in the discussion will be the same as those used in the song, making it easy for the singers to learn the words.

If the subject of a song is understood by a group, if the vocabulary is appropriate, if the melody and rhythm are of the right difficulty, and if the words and music fit together, a song should not be hard to teach. When a class is having trouble learning a song, the teacher would do well to study the song carefully to see what can be done to make it better. Remember, our aim is not to teach songs; our purpose is to use songs to teach something else. The song is merely the instrument that transmits the lesson. The instrument loses its effectiveness if we have to spend time perfecting it. What we need is a simple and efficient tool. We should therefore not waste time rehearsing a song that is too hard. A song that is learned after a period of long, hard practice may finally result in good singing, but it will have been learned by rote and will not have succeeded in teaching anything.

It is not absolutely necessary to have instrumental accompaniment for the singing, but teachers who cannot sing may want instrumental help. Melodic instruments such as song bells or harmonic instruments like the autoharp may be used if there is no piano or pianist available. It is also possible to make tape recordings for use as accompaniment.

One good reason for having "live" accompaniment is that the accompanist can provide introductions for the songs. Since many of our songs are very short, they may be half over before the children start to sing, unless we have prepared our singers by playing an introduction. An introduction also sets the key and the tempo for the singers and gives them practice in listening and watching for the signal to start singing.

For many retarded children, simple accomplishments are to be preferred over fancy ones. Some children lose track of the melody and are not able to sing when the accompaniment is too involved. Others get caught up in the accompaniment and begin singing parts of it instead of the melody.

There are also children who are not well integrated and may be said to be out of harmony with themselves. These people need accompaniments that firmly establish the key through the use of a few basic harmonies and little ornamentation. Tonality means that the tones of the music are related to each other, giving us "key feeling" or a sense of sounds that are drawn toward a center. A confused child should have accompaniments with clear tonal identity to give him a sense of musical order.

The mere addition of a few embellishments and dissonances to an accompaniment can be distracting for some children. But singers who are not distracted by ornamentation will enjoy the variety provided by more complicated and interesting accompaniments.

The accompaniment should be clean, no pedal being preferable to too much. The rhythm needs to be well defined. Above all, the phrasing must be correct and clear. Children will sing even if the accompaniment is phrased poorly or not at all, but they will be able to sing with more meaning if a good accompaniment emphasizes the gathering of words into meaningful groups. If the words and music go together as they should, there is no problem about phrasing; all the pianist has to do is to group the notes the same way the words are grouped.

Playing each song in a different key from the one before will help keep children more alert and interested than they would be if they had to sing song after song in the same key.

An accompanist who plays without music is able to observe the children. If he must have music, he would be wise to cover pictures in the book so that he will not have a crowd of children gathered around him to look at pictures.

A class of hyperactive children can be overstimulated by piano accompaniment. Children like this may appear very happy when they laugh and run excitedly, and the teacher needs to be alert to any sign that they are losing control of themselves. In order to maintain calm for these children, instrumental accompaniment can be omitted, and the group can sit and sing with the teacher in a small circle, preferably in a small room.

Teachers and parents often ask, "Are there any books containing songs appropriate for retarded children?"

There should be no great problem in finding songs for educable children to sing, because simple songs for normal children can be used, sometimes with a few minor changes. Songs with only a few simple words are harder to find, and the teacher who is looking for books of songs for trainables soon finds himself the owner of a huge stack of books, each of which contains one or two suitable songs. It therefore seemed advisable to present this section on how to select, modify, or compose songs, rather than to print a list of books that would soon be out of print or would not have enough suitable songs to make them worth buying. Many of the songs in books do not meet the requirements set up in this chapter because most song books are written for normal children; but it is possible to alter songs, and we can sometimes get ideas from songs we cannot use. New books of songs appear frequently, and teachers may find it profitable to visit a good music store from time to time to look through the latest publications.

## Chapter 6

# MUSIC AND EMOTIONS

MUSIC has been found to be a valuable aid when utilized in conjunction with various forms of therapy—physical, occupational, medical, psychiatric. The addition of music can make a retarded child's therapy sessions more pleasant and, in some cases, more effective.

In a schoolroom situation, the musical emphasis is on teaching, but teachers and music specialists will find that the therapeutic value of music can be used in many ways. Before exploring these possibilities, let us first say a word about the use of music in therapy with children who have severe emotional problems.

We think it wise for teachers to avoid deep involvement in the emotional difficulties of their pupils. This kind of involvement puts one in the position of a psychotherapist, and the music therapist who takes on such a responsibility should be trained in psychotherapy (Darbes, 1961). Those who work with emotionally disturbed children need to consult with psychotherapists who know the students and try to follow their suggestions. Actual therapy is better left in the hands of qualified personnel.

There are times in every school day, however, when music can be used to combat boredom and fatigue, to provide an outlet for hostilities, and to lend a soothing background for quiet times. These periods may be scheduled, or they may be inserted whenever it seems advisable. They may be for the entire class, or they may be for individuals.

A new child who is frightened or shy can often be made more comfortable if some music he knows is sung or played. By trying nursery tunes for young children and playing recordings of popular music, show tunes, TV theme music, and folk songs, we may hit on something the child has heard at home and likes very much. This could help make him feel that school is not all strange and new. Teachers will find it worthwhile to watch children's television programs from time to time and be familiar with commercials that may be just what some new child needs to make him feel at home.

Children who are upset by changes in activity can be prepared beforehand through songs that tell what is going to happen. Timmy was a child who was upset by any change. Whatever he was doing, he went into a series of piercing shrieks when told that it was time to do something else. Anyone who got close to Timmy at such times was sure to come away with a set of bleeding scratches on the back of his hand. The music specialist in the residential school was able to keep her hands intact by carefully preparing Timmy for each change of activity with a song. The day began with a song about opening the curtains to let in the light, followed by a song about removing Timmy's pajamas, then a song about putting on his underwear, his shirt, his pants, his socks, his shoes, washing his face, and on and on. Fortunately, one does not often find a Timmy in a day school, but the same idea can be used with children who need a little help in leaving one activity to go on to another.

When children are so excited that it seems impossible to settle them down, soft, quiet music is not what is needed. The music required is something that equals the mood, tempo, volume, and rhythm of the excited persons. By playing music that is fast, loud, and exciting to match the mood of the wound-up children, we bring them into noisy and agitated, but organized, activity. When the children are thoroughly immersed in the music, the pianist can gradually change the character of the music, leading the group from vigorous rhythms like galloping and running through less active rhythms, such as walking, and into quieter forms, like swaying and tiptoeing and finally, to sitting calmly. This is Altshuler's application of the "iso" principle (Altshuler, 1945).

Because the "iso" maneuver refers to the matching of music to the mood of an individual, it is most effective when used with an individual. It can, however, be used with groups composed of individuals who are sensitive to musical rhythm and are able to respond to it. We have seen teachers give up the "iso" maneuver in disgust because the children did not quiet down after a few minutes. This is a mistake, for it takes time to work off the feelings that cause children to run and yell. A teacher may be able to scream a group into submission, but that leaves an unpleasant aura that is not easily dissipated. The atmosphere is much more relaxed when children are calm and satisfied because they have worked off their tensions.

For one reason or another, a particular song may be disturbing to some child. In such a case, we have to avoid singing that particular song when that child is present.

Six-year-old Dougie became extremely upset one day when his group was playing "The Farmer in the Dell." When the children sang, "The wife takes the child," Dougie broke away from the circle, ran to the teacher, grabbed her, and screamed over and over hysterically, "The wife's not going to take *my* child!" The thought of a wife (whatever that might be) taking a child (Dougie knew he was a child), frightened the insecure little boy, and he screamed until the teacher assured him that the wife certainly would not take away *his* child. Dougie's group never played "The Farmer in the Dell" again.

Patsy was a child who wanted to please her mother but was not able to be the "big girl" her mother wanted her to be. She therefore did not like herself. She happily joined in singing the names of other children, but the class could not sing Patsy's name because she would scream, kick, and cry until they stopped. So, in this case, instead of making sure that no one was left out, we had to remember not to include Patsy in the activity.

There are other children who are soothed by music. No matter how upset they may be, some children quiet down when they hear music. Less frequently, one finds a child who roars, cries, and bites when disturbed, but who calms down immediately when he hears one certain piece of music. The teacher can easily circumvent some unpleasant scenes by using music with this kind of child, but he must be careful not to use it in such a way that he provides a restful musical background for the child's fantasy life.

Some children enjoy acting out stories they have heard. Others make up their own stories, using original lyrics that reveal their thoughts or feelings. We find children like this more often among educable children than among trainables, probably because they have more language ability, imagination, and creativity. Using fantasies to portray thoughts and feelings may be difficult for trainable children, but they can get a degree of emotional release through vocal, instrumental, and motor activity.

A school day contains many similar instances in which music can be used to make things run smoothly for a group or to help an individual feel better. More examples of this kind of work will be found in other parts of the book.

## Chapter 7

# MUSIC AND PHYSICAL COORDINATION

THE most obvious characteristic of coordinated physical movement is rhythm. It seems natural for human beings to move
rhythmically, just as involuntary functions like the respiration and
heartbeat normally operate rhythmically.

Where rhythm is absent, movement is uncoordinated; where
movement is uncoordinated, performance is inefficient. A basketball
player who dribbles unrhythmically, a carpenter who hammers
unrhythmically, or a gardener who rakes unrhythmically cannot
perform competently.

Rhythmic activities with music can be very helpful in the
development of muscular strength and control. Most of the activities
discussed in this chapter can be done by groups, but they are better
done individually if the pupils are very poorly coordinated. Some
children can only move at one speed, and it is necessary for us to
play music at the tempo natural to them. Merely slowing down the
music for these people is not enough. Unless the tempo is suited exactly to their movements, they will have to ignore the music, and we
do not want to encourage inattention in any of our children. The
teacher will have to decide how much individual work can be done
without boring those who have to wait for their turns. The best solution, of course, is to have private sessions with children who need a
great deal of help so that the music specialist can devote complete attention to each of them.

There are children who cannot move in time to music but who
can hear changes in tempo. These children appear to have no feeling
for rhythm, but they move faster when the musical tempo is stepped
up, and they slow down when the music slows down. They apparently hear and feel the beat but are unable to match their movements
to it. Though such a child may not be in synchronization with the
music, he is trying to follow the beat, and his movements may
therefore be better controlled than they are normally. In some cases,
a child's movements to music are almost unbelievably improved over
his movements without music.

To help a child who does not move in time with the music, the pianist should join in with music after the child has started and set his own tempo. After he has learned how it feels to move with the musical beat, the child may be able to adjust to slightly faster or slower tempos.

When we are giving attention to one child at a time, it is a good idea to mix in group work once in a while so that the class will not become bored while waiting for their turns. Some groups are mature enough to wait and watch with interest, and all groups will find waiting easier if they can sing the music used for body rhythms.

Since our classes are confined within walls, many gross motor activities will have to be patterned into a circle or oval. While some children do this naturally, others cut across the room to the opposite wall and stay there because they cannot go any farther, some start in one direction and then shift to another and another, and still others go around in such tight circles that they are almost spinning. If several children like these are moving around at the same time, the result can be very messy.

There are a few things we can do to help those children who cannot direct their movements into a large circular pattern. A circle can be painted on the floor, and the children can be asked to follow the line. Some children are unable to follow a single line but are able to walk between two lines; for them, we can paint a second circle inside or outside the first to form a track that is eight to twelve inches wide. If there are objections to painting the floor, bright plastic tape may be stuck on the floor to outline the track. This is easily done by first drawing the circles or ovals with pencil. Then, what will become the inner edge of the tape is carefully stuck along the outer side of the pencil outline for one circle. Each time a foot or two of tape has been set in place, go back and press it down flat. The plastic tape will stretch and stick smoothly to the floor. Cloth tape is not as elastic as plastic tape and may leave wrinkles; it is also easier for children to peel off.

A child who does not stay on the track can sometimes be helped if we have him crawl around the track on his hands and knees. It may be that he is more aware of the track when he sees it so close to his face; in any case, it often happens that the child can walk or run on the track after he has crawled around it once.

The child with visual problems is sometimes helped by bright spots of color on a few places along the track; even though he cannot follow the track exactly, he may be able to find these bright spots so that he at least has places from which he can start and on which he can stop.

A teacher may find that some children move better in one direction around the circle than in the other and that a few can only go in one direction. If someone in the class can only go in one direction, the rest of the class may be asked to move in that direction too. If there are several who cannot go in the direction preferred by the majority, we can have them perform together and let the others perform as a separate group. A child who seems awkward or who is having difficulties can sometimes do better if we have him try going counter to the direction in which he has been moving.

Persons who go around in tight little circles will never be able to do anything like walking, running, galloping, tiptoeing, or skipping as long as they continue to spin around in one spot. If they are not able to move around a track, they can be asked to go around the outside of a circle of chairs.

A child who is beginning to master one of the gross motor exercises should take his turn after someone who can do it well. If he sees people doing it incorrectly, he may think he should do it that way too, or he may simply forget what the correct way is. He should also have a short turn so that he can do it correctly and finish before he tires and makes mistakes. If he feels cheated because his turn is short, he can be given a second turn later.

The motor activities described below can be modified, added to, or combined to form a variety of movements to use in designing a program for the improvement of physical coordination. Special equipment can be used to help children who have difficulty moving their bodies in any particular way. Examples will be given as we come to them. There are rather elaborate pieces of equipment available for classes in physical education, and any school with money to spare could make teachers very happy by acquiring some gym apparatus, but it is possible to do a great deal without expensive equipment. Teachers should also remember that use of purchased equipment does not have to be confined to those activities described in the instructions issued by the manufacturer.

In helping children with muscular control, we have to remember, as in everything else, that a child cannot do anything that is beyond his present stage of development. It is easy to demand too much of a child if he looks reasonably well coordinated, so the teacher needs to watch closely to determine whether the child is unable to perform a particular movement because he is inattentive, lazy, stubborn, teasing, or incapable. If the reason is one or more of the first four, the teacher's job is to get around or through those obstacles. If the reason is incapability, the child should not be expected to be successful, though he should be allowed the fun of trying if he wants to do it.

The music room floor must be kept as clean as possible. It is bad enough when children play on a dirty floor, but it is worse when we keep a dirty floor and order children to crawl or roll on it.

Some of the following exercises are more effective when done without shoes. Depending upon the skills that have already been mastered and those that are being learned, taking off the shoes, putting them on, tying laces, or buckling straps can be sung about and made a part of the day's musical program so that time spent in taking off and putting on shoes is not wasted.

Many of the motions can be done to songs. This serves a number of purposes. Those persons who have few language skills can learn new words by associating words with actions. Some will find rhythmic motion easier when done to rhythmic speech. Others will be able to speak more rhythmically when speaking while moving.

We have used a few descriptive names such as the bear walk or the duck walk. In talking to children, we avoid such expressions as, "Walk like a bear," or "Take giant steps." Children who are old enough and experienced enough may understand what is meant by the bear walk, duck walk, or giant steps, and the teacher can use those terms as long as the children do not feel that such talk is babyish.

CRAWLING. In crawling, the body is prostrate on the floor and is dragged along by a propellant motion of the arms. Most children in school have progressed beyond crawling, but many of them can use the exercise for the arms. A good way to do this is to put casters on a 12″ × 30″ board and place the board under the body to support the trunk and legs. The casters should not be too close to the edges lest a child run over his own fingers. Taller children may need longer boards so that their knees are kept off the floor and prevented from helping the arms in propelling the body. Well oiled rubber casters will roll easily and keep down the noise level.

CREEPING. This is moving on hands and knees.

CLAPPING. This can be done to any music. Variations are to clap with the hands over the head or with arms extended in front.

SWINGING ARMS. Music in six-eight is good for swinging the arms up over the head and down again. Children who cannot get the idea of raising and lowering their arms can sometimes do better if they hold a rod (rhythm stick) in front of them with both hands and raise and lower the rod without bending their elbows.

WALKING. There are many different ways to walk, and the character of the music should vary to suit each style of walking. For ordinary walking, any music in four-four time with a regular rhythm will do. A drum beat can be used effectively to accompany walking exercises. To accompany a march, we can use music with a more vigorously accented beat. Children who stomp their feet hard on each beat can sometimes be loosened up by a march in six-eight time. Conversely, those with a poorly defined beat can often move with more precision to a four-count rhythm. Occasionally, we find a child with a tendency to put more weight on one foot. (We are not speaking of a child with a physical defect.) Such a child, if he has a good feeling for the beat, can sometimes be helped to even out his walk by walking to a march in three-four time.

Norwegian

Since the accent in the music comes on every third beat, the child (because he has two feet, not three) will feel the accent on one side and then on the other—LEFT, right, left, RIGHT, left, right, LEFT, right, left, RIGHT, left, right.

Children who are distracted or seem unaware of what they are doing while they walk can be asked to stamp their feet on every step. Hearing and feeling their feet as they stamp keeps their attention on their walking.

Another walking exercise is to take long steps, taking time after each step to get ready for the next. The music may be very slow and heavy, or it can be less slow with steps taken several beats apart. Saying or singing words rhythmically can make this easier; the class might say something like, "Step and wait. Step and wait," taking a step as they say, "Step."

Walking backward can present problems if a child is afraid and has to keep turning to see where he is going. One way to help a child who is afraid is to have an adult walk backward right behind him. Another way is to have several children hold hands and walk backward together. The frightened child, of course, should be between two other children.

Lifting the knees high while walking gives practice in maintaining balance. Children who tend to drag their feet can make good use of this exercise. The music will have to be a little slower than for ordinary walking. There are children who cannot imitate this type of walking and have to learn by some other means. Some can do it if a piece of brightly colored tape is stuck on each knee; the child raises each knee until he can see the tape. Others may have to hold one or both hands out in front of themselves and lift each knee until it hits a hand. If the child stoops over to see the tape or to touch his knees, he is obviously not getting the idea; so forget it and try something else.

Another way to get a child to lift his feet is to have him step over the rungs of a ladder that has been placed on the floor. The trouble with using a real ladder is that the rungs may be too far apart for some children. If a ladder is made for this purpose, be sure that there is enough space between rungs for a child's foot to step into easily. Instead of using circular rungs, use flat steps that are of the same width as the sidepieces of the ladder. For example, if the sidepieces are twelve-foot lengths of one-by-four, make the steps of one-by-four also. Then, when the ladder is placed on the floor, all its parts will be touching the floor. With circular rungs, there is a space between the rung and the floor, and children may hook their toes on the rung and fall.

If a child cannot walk by placing one foot in each space but steps over a rung with one foot and then lifts the other foot over to join the first, notice which foot goes over first. If a child always steps first with his right foot, it may be that he can shift his weight to his left foot and step with his right, but cannot shift his weight to the right foot and step with the left.

It would be extremely difficult, if not impossible, for a child who steps over the crosspieces of our ladder in the manner just described to alternate his feet and put only one foot into each space. Before asking him to try such an advanced task, the teacher should have him practice the way he naturally wants to do it, then teach him to do it the same way but leading with the opposite foot. When the child can walk the ladder placing either the left foot or the right foot first, he is ready to try one foot in each space.

A child who can only get a foot over a rung by clinging to the teacher is not ready to use the ladder, though he may try to do it if he wishes. The teacher will have to be careful that the child does not hurt himself in the attempt.

The child who walks with his feet far apart may be given practice in getting his feet closer together and in taking longer strides. Carpeting cut into 6″ × 8″ rectangles can be placed steppingstone fashion on the floor. The carpet pieces should have latex or other nonskid backing to keep them from sliding around, and should be of a color that makes them stand out against the floor. The rectangles are positioned about the way the child usually steps, both in distance between the feet and in length of stride. Gradually, they can be brought closer, left and right, and the stride lengthened, until the gait is closer to normal. The carpeting is better than marks on the floor because the child can tell by feel when he is on it and when he has missed it. This is even better when done with the shoes off. The pieces can be any size that is convenient to make as long as they are not too small for the children's feet to step on comfortably or so big that it takes no effort to place the feet on them.

Where they can be left more or less permanently, self-adhesive carpet tiles cut into convenient sizes can be stuck to the floor as steppingstones for children to walk on. Another set might be arranged with the tiles placed far enough apart so that it is necessary to hop from tile to tile. For training purposes, it is better to use carpet pieces that can be picked up and arranged to suit each child who uses them.

Walking on a line is good for children who can do it. For those who have problems with that, a heavy cord stretched across the floor can be easier to follow, as they can feel the cord under their feet.

A balance beam set high enough to prevent anyone from walking with one foot on the floor and one foot on the beam is enjoyed by many children. Those who are afraid to be off the floor might use a board placed right on the floor. One who is extremely frightened of heights might need to start out with a board as wide as twelve inches, even if it is on the floor. As he gains confidence, he can use a narrower board.

RUNNING. There is a difference between running and fast walking. In running, there is an instant in each step when both feet are off the floor. Sometimes, a child who does not run can be helped if he is pulled by the hand. Though we think of running as being fast, there are children who take long, slow running steps, and the pianist must take care to match their tempos.

SWAYING. Music in six-eight is well suited to swaying. The child stands with his feet apart and moves his entire body from side to side without bending his knees. The teacher can help by standing in front of the child, with his hands high on the child's arms. By swaying far to one side and then to the other, he can sometimes cause the child to sway with him. If the child stumbles about when the teacher does this, he may be standing with his feet too close together, or he may not have the necessary balance. Some have better luck if they stand on squares of brightly colored paper; they seem to get the idea by watching their feet as they alternately lift them off the squares. Since paper tears easily, twelve-inch squares of carpeting may be more practical. With shoes removed, the children will have the added advantage of being able to feel the carpeting.

TIPTOEING. The difficult part of tiptoeing is getting up on the toes. Once a child can get up and stay up on his toes, the rest is simple. If a child does not get the idea from seeing someone else tiptoe, he may have to be shown what to do. The teacher stands in front of the child with his hands on the child's shoulders and suddenly rises on his toes as he says, "Up!" Often, the child will see that the teacher is standing taller, and will also get up on his toes without even thinking about it. If he still does not know what to do, the teacher should step back far enough so that the child can see both his own feet and the teacher's feet and repeat the maneuver. This method is more effective than holding up the child as he walks. When the child rises on his toes by himself, he knows what he has done because he can feel it in his muscles. When the teacher holds up the child, it is only the teacher who feels a strain in his muscles.

Light, staccato music will convey the idea of walking lightly on tiptoe. Played a little faster, the music can be used for running on tiptoe.

JUMPING. Children who like to jump can jump fast and keep going for a long time, but it is also good to have them slow down and jump on signal. Those who need to get set before each jump can jump on the off beat to music such as the following:

(jump)  (jump)  (jump)  (jump)  (jump)

When demonstrating how to jump, the teacher will need to jump as high as possible so that he is obviously (to the retarded observer) off the floor. Holding the child's hands while jumping is also a help at times. Children who take off from one foot will sometimes jump with both feet if the adult says, "Two feet," even though they seem to have no understanding of numbers. We offer no explanation for this; we have just found that it sometimes works.

Some children jump forward instead of jumping straight up and down; as they do this, one foot gets out in front of the other, and soon they are galloping instead of jumping. To prevent this, squares can be marked off on the floor and the children invited to try jumping without stepping outside the squares.

Variations of the jumping theme are to jump forward, backward, or to the sides. Places to jump may be marked on the floor. Bentley suggests using old bicycle tires (Bentley, 1970), and these may be easier to see. It also gives practice in jumping over something. Experimentation will show what size tires are best for the group.

Blocks of wood can be used for jumping over. A two-foot length of one-by-four is easy to jump because it is only an inch high. Another block can be placed on it to make a higher obstacle to jump. The blocks can be piled higher and higher as long as the children can jump over them.

One way to do this is to put a block across the circular track described earlier. The children stand in line behind the obstacle. At a signal, the first child in line jumps over the block and then follows the track to the end of the line of children. When each child has had a turn, another block is added to the pile. To keep the music from getting boring as well as to show that it is another person's turn, the song can be pitched a half tone higher each time it is played and sung:

On your mark, get    set,    go!

On your    mark, get    set, go!

On your mark, get    set,    go!

GALLOPING. Children who are just learning to gallop may have trouble when they try to gallop in a circle. They may find it easier to go straight across the room. A child who seems unable to keep one foot ahead of the other can sometimes do it if he is asked to shift position and try with the other foot in front.

SLIDING. A slide differs from a gallop in that the movement is to the side, not forward. People who have trouble moving sideways can do it more easily by holding a partner's hands. Those who simply are not ready for this may do it very slowly — step, slide; step, slide — to get the idea of moving to the side. To make sure that they move sideways, we can let them do it with partners or on a plank placed on the floor.

SKIPPING. When children gallop upon being shown how to skip, they can be allowed to go ahead and gallop since the music will fit the gallop. If a galloping child occasionally gets the other foot in front, he can sometimes be helped to alternate his feet if we call out to him, "Two feet!" Again, we do not know why this works, but it sometimes does. A child who skips on one foot and walks on the other may be helped if we say, "Hop," as each foot goes down.

HOPPING. One might suppose that it is necessary to be able to balance oneself on one foot before learning to hop. This is not always the case. Some children can stand on one foot but are unable to hop on it. Others hop because they cannot keep their balance on one foot and would fall over unless they keep hopping. The only suggestion we can make for teaching children to hop is to let them try now and then. Letting the child hold on to something or someone does not seem to help, as the child then puts his weight on the support instead of on his own foot.

BEAR WALK. This is different from creeping in that the child walks on his hands and feet with his knees straight, instead of on his hands and knees.

DUCK WALK. Walk in a squatting position with hands at the waist. Some people can do better with their hands on their knees. It is easier done on the toes than with the feet flat on the floor.

There are countless other motions that can be made to music: spinning, bending and unbending, stooping and standing, sitting and standing, turning the body from side to side, opening and closing the hands, bending and unbending the arms, getting up on the toes and down again, turning the head from side to side, rolling on the floor, somersaulting, and any others that occur to the teacher or that children do spontaneously. Some bodily rhythms can be done while lying on the back: raising and lowering the legs, sliding the legs apart and together, sliding the arms away from and back to the sides, sitting up and lying down.

Bentley presents many interesting activities for movement education (Bentley, 1970). By selecting those best suited to our groups and combining them with music, we can add variety and fun to our rhythm program.

Some body rhythms can be done with partners or in groups. Two children can sit tailor fashion on the floor, facing each other and holding hands. They then rock backward and forward, each partner pulling when it is his turn to rock back. Some children do this better with their knees bent and their feet braced against their partners' feet. Other things that can be done holding a partner's hands are swaying, squatting and standing, and sliding. Of course, all movements like walking and running can be done with a partner.

Games can be made using these motions, and simple dances are made by combining the movements that the group can do well. Examples are given in another chapter.

Many of our retardates ascend and descend stairs with difficulty.

Some are terribly frightened, especially when they look down a long flight of stairs. The first thing we can do is to let them get used to walking up and down just a few steps. For this purpose, a set of steps—a platform with three or four steps going down from each end—with bannisters on both sides is very useful. The bannisters should not more than thirty-six inches apart, and if the children are very little, they may have to be even closer together. Both the tread and the riser must be of standard measurements, and the bannisters should be at regulation height. Little steps with low bannisters may be cute, but big children will not be able to use them; besides, all children have to live with adult-size stairs wherever they go. (We are speaking of equipment for use in our own programs and do not mean that little steps or little furniture should never be used.)

Having bannisters on both sides makes it simpler to go up and down with only one foot on each tread. Let those who place both feet on each tread go up and down that way. The next time, let them do the same thing but with the other foot leading. When they are comfortable leading with either foot, they are ready to try one foot on each step. Those who need to may hold on to both bannisters. Those who need only one can use either bannister, depending upon which hand they want to use. They should then be taught to use the other bannister so that they will be able to climb stairs anywhere, even though the bannister is not on the side where they would like it to be. If a child is extremely frightened, place one side of the steps next to a wall; most staircases have a wall on one side, anyway.

The simplest thing to sing for the step exercise is, "Up, up, up, up, up," and "Down, down, down, down, down," going up and down the first five notes of the scale. Depending upon the number of steps and how long it takes a person to move, we might use only three notes of the scale or the entire scale. We may even have to sing, "Up," several times on each note for someone whose attention wanders or who needs time to work up enough energy and determination to negotiate the next step.

When we cannot make our pupils understand what we want them to do, everyday objects and furniture can often be employed to get them to make the motions. If, for instance, we want them to bend or squat, we can put a box of small blocks on the floor near a shelf and have a child pick up one block at a time and place it on the shelf. The next child can pick one block at a time off the shelf and put it in the box. Or, if we want a stretching and bending exercise, the box of blocks may be set on the floor near a high shelf so that the child has to stretch in order to put the block on the shelf. An adult may have to help by putting one block at a time into the box for a child who tries to pick up all the blocks at once.

A similar device can be used for getting children to twist around from side to side. A child stands with his back to a table. With his right hand, he takes a small block from the side of the table to his left and turns to set it down on the right side. His feet should remain still. When he has transferred all the blocks to the right side, he uses his left hand to bring them back again. If he has a hard time using only one hand, he can keep the other hand in a pocket or on his head or hold on to his belt or whatever else the teacher can think of to try.

One piece of homemade equipment is good for using the arms rhythmically. Bore holes into the base of a good bicycle pump and screw or bolt it to a board large enough to stand on. This eliminates the problem of having to hold the pump down with the feet. To the end of the hose, tape the noise-making part of a toy horn (a bicycle horn is good). As the air is pumped out, the horn toots. The entire horn can be used, but many children find it distracting.

A 12″ × 12″ board on casters can be sat on and propelled by the feet. Casters on all wheeled boards should not be too close to the edges of the boards.

A tricycle can be used as a kind of exercise machine. Turn the tricycle over so that the handlebars are on the floor and the front wheel spins freely. Hook the handlebars on the front legs of a chair. A child sits in the chair, holding on to the seat, and pedals the tricycle with his feet. He can learn to pedal both forward and backward. If you are trying to teach a child to ride a tricycle instead of spinning the wheel with his hands or just walking around with it, you may not want to do this exercise.

Playing rhythm instruments is another pleasant way of doing exercises for physical coordination. Making a wide sidearm swing at a large drum, taking a well-aimed bing at a xylophone bar, rapping a tambourine, bringing finger cymbals together with precision — these and all the other movements required in playing instruments are useful for people who need muscular development.

Children with good rhythmic speech can sometimes move their bodies more rhythmically if they speak or sing as they move. One of the simplest things to do is to have the child sing his name up or down the scale as he walks:

Gin    Tu   Wong,    Gin    Tu   Wong,    Gin    Tu   Wong,    Gin    Tu   Wong,

Teachers who use music freely can include movement development work in their daily schedules. Much of this work can also be done at unscheduled times, such as during playground or gym periods. A teacher encouraging a hesitant child to climb the ladder to a slide by singing, "Theresa climbs up, and up, and up," may soon be surrounded by children who want to climb up, and up, and up. A music specialist is not needed except, perhaps, to demonstrate what can be done. Remember, a nonsinging teacher has no excuse for neglecting rhythmic activity. Anyone who has rhythmic speech can say, "Bounce the ball, bounce the ball," or "Jump, clap, jump, clap."

We have presented a few ideas for using music with motor activity. Try some of our suggestions if they seem practical, and do some creative thinking to work out useful activities for your own classes.

## Chapter 8

# MUSIC IN SOCIAL DEVELOPMENT

THE delayed social development of a retarded child is often further impeded by conditions in his environment, and those conditions, conversely, are sometimes caused by the child's retardation. Parents of other children, for example, may be afraid to let their children play with a child who is obviously very different from other children. They may feel that such a child could physically harm their own children because he is older and bigger and does not know his own strength. Other parents are afraid that their children will pick up bad habits from the retarded child. Many people have such notions even when their children are worse bullies and have worse habits than any retarded child they have ever seen.

Normal childen of the same age may find that the retarded child's interests, skills, and behavior are too infantile to please them. Some of them may ridicule the retarded child because of his poor physical coordination or his poor speech. Even the child's own family can baby him because of his handicap, thus hampering his emotional and social development. Other families may reject the retarded member, depriving him of the opportunity to interact with those closest to him.

Fortunately, not all children are burdened with additional problems of this kind. Some are blessed with sensible parents who, besides providing them with warm family relationships, let them participate in the normal experiences of everyday living including those outside the home such as shopping, traveling, dining, and playing with other children.

So as in everything else, the children who come to our schools differ in their social attainments. The most immature must first establish their own identities and become conscious of themselves as individuals apart from others. They must then learn to establish relationships with other persons, progressing from a mere awareness of people, to communication and interaction with them.

Placing a child in the proper school group automatically gives him the opportunity to become involved in classroom experiences that aid his social development, but most children will need the additional help of planned activities directed toward social growth. Many of these can be set to music, and we offer a few examples in

71

the rest of this chapter. The children who need much help in developing socially are usually young, and the songs are made very simple so that they may be picked up quickly and easily. They can be even simpler with the words being sung on only one or two tones.

To help socially immature children increase their awareness of themselves, we can use their names often in speaking or singing to them. If this is to be effective, it will have to be done when the teacher is working with that child alone. Even when there is a group present, each child should know when the teacher is speaking directly to him. The teacher can help by looking at the child and by touching him or even by holding his head if necessary in order to get eye-to-eye contact.

The simplest musical thing to do is to sing names. The natural "calling" melody is best for this purpose:

Though as a general rule we prefer to limit single syllables to one tone, it is so natural to use two tones in calling that for some names we give two tones to one syllable:

By adding a few words that tell something about the child, we help to identify him further. These songs are sung while the child is actually performing an act — not before or after he has done it — to call his attention to his own involvement in the activity:

Don - ny    is    tak - ing    off    his    shoes.

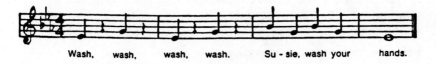

Wash,    wash,    wash,    wash.    Su - sie, wash your    hands.

If we want a child to see that he is a person and that someone else is another person, we can use the names of both people when they are doing something together:

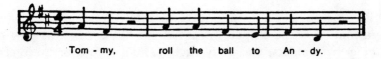

Tom - my,    roll    the    ball    to    An - dy.

When a child can say his name, we can give him practice in identifying himself to others:

Teacher:                Child:

What's    your    name?    Jo - ey.

The child who persists in singing both question and answer is obviously not ready for this kind of exchange.

Those who are learning their last names could use something like this:

Teacher:                Child:

What's    your    last    name?    De - mas.

When a child has learned to respond to his name, we can teach him to greet other people whose names he knows:

For the example above, Willie stands in front of the others. When the teacher sings, "Hi, Bobby," Willie waves to Bobby. He waves to each child as the teacher sings "Hi" to them. If he can, he says "Hi" or "Hello" with the teacher. A child who can say the names of other children can sing with the teacher or by himself.

Children who are a little more advanced will be able to take turns greeting and returning greetings:

People who have not yet learned to work with others can be given opportunities to participate in parallel activities such as singing, playing instruments, and body rhythms. There will be no interaction between children, but all the members of the group will be doing the same things in proximity to each other. Eventually, they may come to realize that others are doing the same thing they are doing.

Simple games that demand only that the players sit on chairs in a circle and do what everyone else is doing are good at this level. For example, the teacher begins opening and closing his hands, turning his head from side to side, clapping his hands, or any one of many possible rhythmic motions while singing or saying words that tell what he is doing. The children imitate the action as they become aware of what is happening. If there are some who do not join in, an adult may invite the child to do so, and if that is not enough, the adult can help the child make the motions. The children should be given time, however, to notice what is going on and to begin participating on their own.

Stand-up games are possible too. If the children are given to running off by themselves, it is best to have short activities in which hands can be held from beginning to end. Two examples are given below:

Stamp, stamp, stamp. Stamp, stamp, stamp. Now we make a bow.

Stamp, stamp, stamp. Stamp, stamp, stamp. Now we make a bow.

Walk, walk, walk, walk. Jump, jump, jump.

Walk, walk, walk, walk. Jump, jump, jump.

The teacher should take advantage of every opportunity to make an ordinary occurrence into a learning experience. For instance, if we are letting children take turns playing a drum, rather than taking the drum when Stan is finished playing, and giving it to someone else, we can say, "Stan, give the drum to Linda." If Stan does not respond, we shall want to find out whether he knows who Linda is by asking him, "Where is Linda?" If he indicates in any way that he knows Linda, we can repeat, "Give the drum to Linda." Should there still be no response, we may take Stan over to Linda and say, "This is Linda. Give the drum to Linda." It may even be necessary to help the boy hold the drum out to Linda.

It is usually very young children who need as much help as this. With children who are even less socially developed, we would, after giving a child a very short turn with the instrument, simply walk him over to another child, take the drum, and hand it to the other child while saying, "Give the drum to Linda."

Another way of helping a child emerge as an individual is to make him aware of his body and its parts so that he recognizes himself as a well-defined individual with hands, feet, head, and all the rest. We can sing about what the child is doing with his hands—"Wash your hands," "Clap your hands," or "Shake your hands." Clapping and shaking the hands are effective exercises because they are kinesthetic experiences; the children can feel their hands as they clap them or shake them.

Some teachers dislike having children shake their hands or rock to music because they feel that shaking and rocking, being characteristic of many retardates, should be stopped rather than encouraged. We have often played music to match the rocking of children who are habitual rockers, and we have found that many of them stop rocking when the music stops. If we have them shake their hands or rock only when they are asked to do it to music, nonshakers and nonrockers are not likely to become shakers and rockers.

The hands are easy for children to learn about since they are out where they can be seen and are used frequently throughout the day. The feet, because they are usually hidden inside socks and shoes, are not as familiar. Children who are not yet aware of their own bodies should be able to see and feel their feet when the teacher talks about them. In a residential school, it is a simple matter to talk or sing about the feet while the child is dressing or bathing. In a day school, it might be done when children are dressing or undressing at rest period. The teacher can hold the child's foot and sing something very simple like the following:

Foot.     Foot.     Da - vid's     foot.

Children who know there is a foot inside the shoe can have the experience of hearing and feeling their feet as they stamp to music. Another way of making a child conscious of his feet is to attach bells to his shoes. Take an elastic band (three-fourths inch wide) and cut off a piece about six inches long. Overlap the ends and sew them together so that you have a large ring. Sew a large jingle bell to the elastic ring. You will need two of these. They are slipped over the toes of the children's shoes. A bell jingles each time a foot strikes the floor, drawing the child's attention to his feet. The rhythmic sound also makes walking to music easier.

These bells may be used on the hands or wrists when the idea is to have jingling bells, but they are not useful for hands in the same way that they are good on the feet. Movements of the feet are limited when people are standing, because of the need to maintain balance.

The hands, however, are free to move randomly and frequently or even constantly, intentionally or unintentionally. Putting bells on the hands, therefore, sets up a patternless jingling that is difficult to relate to any specific motion.

After they have learned some body parts, the children can play a simple game in which the teacher asks them to identify a body part, and they respond by pointing:

Where is your arm? Where is your head?

Later, they can play a game which teaches them that other people have arms and legs and heads too:

Ra - mo - na. Where is Gwen - do - lyn's foot?

The teacher sings the question, and Ramona goes over and points to Gwendolyn's foot. When doing this with facial features, the teacher needs to watch carefully so that no one is poked in the eye.

Children who have more language skills enjoy the following game:

Old French Song

Ev' - ry - bod - y, Lis - ten, ev' - ry - bod - y.

Ev' - ry - bod - y, play this game with me.

Put your fin - ger on your head. Put your fin - ger on your head.

On your head, on your head, Oh - - -, oh - - -.

Those who can sing the song may take turns being the leader. Older children have fun doing it the way it is done in the original French, adding another body part each time and repeating all those which have already been sung.

> Everybody, listen, everybody.
> Everybody, play this game with me.
> Put your finger on your chin.
> Put your finger on your chin.
> On your chin, On your chin,
> On your head, On your head,
> Oh _____, Oh _____.

> Everybody, listen, everybody.
> Everybody, play this game with me.
> Put your finger on your foot.
> Put your finger on your foot.
> On your foot, On your foot,
> On your chin, On your chin,
> On your head, On your head,
> Oh _____, Oh _____.

And so on it continues until all the parts learned have been included in the song. The first two lines are sung as the final lines of the song. It may be necessary to use pictures so that the singers will know in what order to sing the parts of the body. If pictures are used, add the picture of each new part to the left of the others so that they can be read from left to right when they are sung in order.

Often, as a group enters the room, some boy or girl announces with delight, "New shoes!" or "I have a new dress." We can give recognition to these individuals by singing about their new possessions:

New shoes. New shoes. Lau-ra has some new shoes.

In doing this, we strengthen the child's appreciation of himself as an entity—one who is separate from others, one who owns things that belong to him alone. Obviously, there will be infrequent occasions for using this device if we limit our use of it to those times when someone displays a new item of apparel. Besides, a few children receive new things often, while others seldom have anything to show off. To get around this, we sing about each child's belongings, new or old. After singing about Laura's new shoes, we go down the line and sing about everyone's shoes, or about different things that people are wearing:

Socks,    socks,    Bil - ly's    socks.

Children who know colors can sing about Billy's black shoes, Gregory's brown shoes, or Diane's red shoes to the same tune that was used for Laura's new shoes.

There is one game that we can modify in several different ways to fit children who are at various levels of development. The easiest way to play the game may be to have one child stand in the center of a circle, making appropriate motions while the teacher and/or children sing the song. The game is easier to play if the children are seated in chairs.

Sal - ly Thom - son, turn a - round, turn a - round, turn a - round,

Sal - ly Thom - son, turn a - round, Stop and point to Ma - ry.

Children who have some speech can sing the same song with the words of the last two measures changed to "Stop and point your finger." Sally Thomson then points to any person of her choice and asks, "What's your name?" The person to whom she is pointing gives his or her name and takes Sally's place in the middle of the circle.

When they have learned to distinguish between the sexes pretty well, the group can play another variation of the game. The teacher asks whether Sally Thomson is a girl or boy. When it has been decided that Sally is a girl, she stands in the circle while the others sing, "Girl in the middle, turn around." After Sally has pointed to someone and asked, "What's your name?" and received an answer—

"Paul," for example—the teacher asks Sally, "Is Paul a boy or girl?" When Sally has answered correctly, she sits in Paul's chair while Paul stands in the circle and everyone sings, "Boy in the middle, turn around."

A more complicated game is an adaptation of an old circle game. All the children except "It" sit in a circle. The chairs are placed far enough apart so that a person can easily walk between them. While "It" weaves in and out between the chairs, the group sings:

Old Game Song

At this point, David stops walking and stands behind or beside (this must be predetermined) another child. The teacher asks David whether that child is a boy or girl, and after David has answered correctly, everyone sings while David taps the child's shoulder.

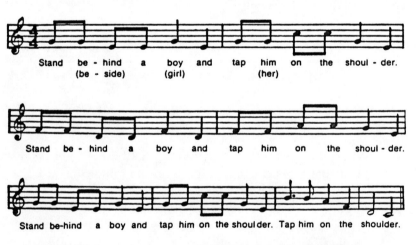

The child who was tapped now becomes "It," and David sits in the vacated chair. Children who cannot weave in and out may walk around the outer side of the circle while the group sings, "Round and round goes _____, Round and round the circle." This game may be combined with a body part game, and the teacher may ask "It" to tap the boy's or girl's arm or head or foot.

The music period provides many opportunities for learning to share. Certain kinds of rhythm and instrumental work can only be done by one or a few at a time, and the others must learn to wait their turns. Some instruments, such as a large drum, can be played by two or more children. Those who enjoy other people have fun sharing the instrument, while those who want things for themselves find that they have to share in order to get a chance to play.

Activities done by couples are a beginning toward cooperative play. The child realizes that he needs a partner if he is to hold someone's hand or tap someone's shoulder, and he learns to seek out a friend who can do things with him. Rhythms like swaying and jumping can be done by two children facing each other and holding hands.

The following is a very easy partner game. A child walks, runs, or gallops to music; the second time the music is played, he takes a partner who walks, runs, or gallops with him. The first child then sits down while the second child takes a turn by himself, then chooses a partner to take a turn around the room with him.

A well-organized rhythm band is good for giving children the idea of contributing a part to the whole. Each participant learns that he cannot play all the time or whenever he chooses to play; he learns that he is missed when he forgets to play; he learns that others have their parts and their times to play; and he eventually learns that when each person does his part well, the result is satisfying for all.

Losing gracefully when playing games is no problem for the retarded child who is not interested in playing or who thinks it is fun to lose or who doesn't know whether he has won or lost. But for the child who *must* win every time, losing is a terrible experience that can bring on tears or tantrums. It is a mistake to let a child like this win every time in order to keep him happy, for he will then be unprepared for the many times in life when he cannot be a winner. A child cannot be shielded from competition as long as he lives among other people, but we can at least help him see that no one wins all the time and that it is not a terrible thing to lose. This means that we may have to "fix" games so that no one child either wins every time or loses every time.

In musical chairs, for example, the teacher takes care not to stop the music when Jerry, who is usually the first one out, obviously has no chance of getting a chair. Or if Debra, who always wins, and Margie are the only two left in the game, the teacher stops the music when Margie is in better position for getting the remaining chair than is Debra. Children who are very anxious to win sometimes put their hands or even their bodies on the chairs in order to have a better chance of getting a chair. To prevent this, the children may be asked to walk with their hands on their heads or to run, skip, gallop, or jump around the chairs instead of walking. If this is not enough, the players may be required to march or run around a circle drawn on the floor so that they cannot get close to the chairs until it is time to sit.

Short games that can be played over and over give more opportunities for the children to see that no one *always* wins. The teacher can also help by starting the next game without taking time to congratulate the winner effusively.

With so many possibilities for incorporating music into a social development program, every music class can be conducted with a positive developmental goal in view. The teacher who is alert to the needs of his pupils will seek and find new musical methods of awakening the group to the pleasures of knowing how to live with others.

Chapter 9

# MUSIC IN TEACHING

LEARNING is best when it is not just painless but actually entertaining. The person of low intelligence, having little motivation for applying himself to learning, is easily bored and distracted and has a greater need for education camouflaged in fun than does the average person. Because he learns slowly over a long period of time, he also needs many different types of amusing activities for each learning unit to ensure the possibility of repetition without boredom. His teacher has the pleasure, and sometimes the problem, of thinking up many interesting ways of presenting the same lesson.

This chapter proposes ideas on how to mix music with teaching to help the teacher augment his repertoire of teaching techniques. These methods are to be used in addition to, not in place of, the regular classroom methods.

## ATTENTION

The attention span of retardates is characteristically short. The younger, the more severely retarded, and those who have never been required to attend to anything will usually have the most difficulty in keeping their attention on the lesson. There are other problems — physical, emotional, neurological — that may contribute to the difficulty. We shall want to discover the reason or reasons for a child's inability to attend, because the way we handle the problem will depend, to some extent, upon those reasons.

Attention is bonded to interest. It is not necessary to repeatedly call attention to something that interests a student, for where interest exists, attention is also alive. To hold a child's attention, the teacher has to keep doing interesting things with interesting material.

Because children attend to things that interest them, some teachers select classroom activities on the basis of the group's interests. This is an excellent procedure if those interests happen to be in things the class should be learning. Unfortunately, however, we often see children doing things they already know how to do, week after week, month after month, and even year after year while the teacher exclaims, "They just *love* to do this!"

Even worse are classes in which the students do things poorly or incorrectly because they are not yet capable of doing them well or correctly while the teacher exclaims, "They just *love* to do this!"

In order to plan an effective program, the teacher has to know what his pupils have already learned and then determine what they must learn next. This determination is to be based on needs and the importance of fulfilling those needs, not on what the class members like to do. *"The content of education cannot be determined by interest. . . . We determine the content of education by its importance"* (Mursell, 1934).

Once the class objectives have been established, the teacher must decide what teaching methods and techniques he should use. *This is the time to consider the children's interests.* Although the selection of learning objectives is not based on interest, the methods employed in teaching should make use of materials and activities that are of special interest to the learners. The wide appeal of music makes it an exceptionally useful teaching instrument.

No matter how clever and intriguing our instructional methods and devices may be, they will not sustain the attention of a child who has reached the limit of his ability to attend. If a child has been allowed to reach this point, he will have lost interest along with his waning attention. For this reason, we ought to change activities while the child is still enjoying his lesson so that he can return to it with enthusiasm the next time.

The rest of this chapter offers examples of the function of music in adding interest to dull lessons and excitement to interesting lessons.

## EXPERIENCE UNITS

An experience unit is a unit of study that is planned to cover a period of days or weeks, depending upon the nature of the unit and the maturity and ability of the children. A unit usually begins with an introductory activity—the experience itself. Experiences that can be repeated (washing hands and faces, cleaning the room, setting the table) are done many times during the unit period. Experiences that cannot be repeated often (circus, farm, restaurant) are relived through dramatizations, pictures, and storytelling. All areas of the educational program are built around the unit theme. The unit ends with a culminating activity—a performance, a party, a display— that brings together everything that has been learned concerning the unit.

Let us take as an example a unit on autumn leaves. Experiences might include watching leaves fall from trees, chasing windblown leaves, picking leaves off the ground, raking leaves, or stuffing leaves into plastic bags for trash collection.

Classroom activities could include things like coloring leaf forms, cutting out paper leaves, counting leaves, identifying leaf colors, pasting cutout leaves onto a picture, acting out the experience, making a picture book of the experience, learning new words related to the experience, waxing leaves, embedding leaves in plastic for use as paperweights, or anything else the teachers think would be good for their classes.

Music activities would consist of songs about leaves and the things the children did with them. Body rhythms could be done to songs about raking, putting leaves into a bag, or picking up leaves.

For a final activity, the pictures, stories, handcrafts, and other items made by the classes could be displayed. Several classes could meet together and have a music session of the unit songs and activities. Or each class might want to invite parents to see and hear all they learned about autumn leaves.

To be most effective, music is applied along with the actual experience. This means that the teacher and music specialist must outline the sequence of activities involved in the experience and have the songs ready before the unit begins.

When singing cannot be done during the new experience, the music must wait until a dramatization or a story of the experience is worked out in the schoolroom. At appropriate places in the dramatization or the depicted experience, songs can be used to reinforce the memory.

After the classroom teacher has made a start, the music specialist can begin talking about the unit, using objects or pictures representing the experience.

Presented below is the order of songs we used for a unit on travel by bus. For several months, the children went to a Boys Club once a week to swim, and therefore had many opportunities for repeating the experience of riding the bus.

Walking to the bus stop
Crossing streets with traffic lights
Looking left and right before crossing
Waiting for the bus
Getting on the bus
Giving fare to driver
Getting token and transfer from driver
Putting token into the box
Sitting in the bus
Putting transfer into pocket
Talking to friends; not to strangers
Watching for stop
Getting off the bus
Giving transfer to second driver

These songs were used while children acted out the procedure. Several fathers from the parents' organization made a large, plywood form that looked like the side of a bus. They cut out windows and doors and painted it to look just like the real city buses. The bus was made so that it could stand up away from the wall with room for the driver's and passengers' seats behind it. A coin box was put beside the driver's seat. "Bus stop" signs and traffic lights were made, and tokens, transfers, and a cap for the driver were acquired.

For the traffic light song, a child stood at the traffic light with a flashlight to shine through the red, yellow, or green circle at the right time in the song. The children who were to ride the bus watched for the green light before crossing the street. The entire sequence was carried out in the same fashion, and everyone enjoyed it because it was the reenactment of a very familiar experience.

Toy instruments can be used with songs for appropriate sound effects. In the bus unit, for instance, instruments could provide sounds for the token dropping into the coin box and for the honking of the bus horn.

There are times when songs should be taught before the children have had the experience. Teachers may want to use songs to help them prepare children for something that is to happen.

One such experience was a two-week camp, which was held at the end of the regular school year. For children who had been to camp before, the unit was review as well as preparation. For new campers, the unit provided a way of learning something of what camp was about so that the experience would not be totally strange and frightening.

The daily camp schedule was followed in the music sessions. Songs to be sung at camp were introduced and sung while the children acted them out. Some of the daily activities sung about were getting up, morning routines, breakfast, making beds, cleaning rooms, lunch, supper, campfire, and bedtime. Besides these, there were songs about things that might or might not happen every day: swimming, boating, hiking, riding donkeys, popping corn.

The songs and other preparatory activities thus served as familiar and reassuring old friends in a new environment.

## GAMES

Many games can be modified or invented to be used as teaching devices. A good example is the game of musical chairs. Here are a few possibilities.

1. Play in the usual manner but with two rows of chairs back to back instead of one row with alternate chairs facing the same way. Remind inattentive children to listen to the music.

2. All chairs have identical pictures or pieces of colored tape stuck to the front of the chair backs. Instead of removing chairs one by one, the pictures or tapes are removed one by one, and the object is to get a chair that still has a picture on it. Special pictures may be used for special days: hearts, eggs in baskets, pumpkins or witches, turkeys, Santa Claus or Christmas trees. Pictures are prepared with pieces of Scotch® tape that go across the pictures and extend beyond the sides. The extensions hold the pictures on the chairs. When not in use, the pictures may be kept on a sheet of wax paper. Chairs may be placed in a row all facing the same way so that the teacher can stand the children in front of the chairs and show them the pictures.

3. Play as above but replace removed pictures with one of something else. For example, if all chairs have a picture of a car at the start of the game, the children are instructed to find a chair with the picture of a car. When one car is removed, it might be

replaced by a house. The next one might be replaced by the picture of a dog. Before each march, the teacher may need to remind the players to find a chair with a car on it. The game is for practice and should only be used with material that has been learned well.

4. Another variation of the above is to use pictures of things in one category. As an example, we might take things to eat. All chairs would have pictures of different kinds of food, and each picture that is removed would be replaced by one of something inedible—toy, bus, book—and the players try to sit in a chair that has a picture of something to eat.

5. We can also play the game with colors. Let us say orange is the color we are going to look for. As each orange piece is removed from the chairs, another color is substituted.

The same can be done with forms, numerals, letters, or words.

"Looby Loo" can be made into a game for practicing *in front* and *in back*. After moving in a circle, the players stop to sing and act out, "I put my hand in front. I put my hand in back."

Here is one for visual memory. "It" is blindfolded, and another child hides. The blindfold is removed while everyone sings:

Who is gone? Who is gone? Gre - ta, tell us who is gone.

"It" looks around and figures out who is missing. This can be done with objects if people are too easy, and the words can be changed to "What is gone?"

A good blindfold can be made by taking a mask that covers only the eyes and putting tape over both the front and back of the eye slits. Tie one end of an elastic cord to each side of the mask, and the cord can be stretched to fit behind the head of the person to be blindfolded. If someone in the class has a head so large that the cord will not stretch far enough, tie one cord to each side of the mask and join the other two ends in a bow. Then, for the person with the large head, the bow can be untied and tied again so that the cord fits comfortably around his head.

For practice in auditory discrimination, "It" covers his eyes (some children will have to be blindfolded) while the teacher or another child picks up an instrument and plays it. When the instrument has been returned to the table, "It" opens his eyes and tries to choose the one he heard. This procedure may be repeated if necessary.

In the next game, the players have to watch "It" in order to find out what to do. "It" sits facing the group and does some bodily rhythm to the song:

Eve - ry - bod - y, look at Ped - ro. Eve - ry - bod - y, look at Ped - ro.

Eve - ry - bod - y, look at Ped - ro; Do what Ped - ro's do - ing.

The song is played a second time while everyone does what "It" is doing.

Other games can be found under various headings elsewhere in these pages. It is a good thing to use games mainly for review and practice of material already learned. A game can neither be effective nor entertaining if the players have to struggle to understand what they are doing.

Chapter 10

# MUSIC IN LANGUAGE
# AND
# SPEECH DEVELOPMENT

P ARENTS of retarded children often express concern over the slow development of communicative skills in their children. We do not usually hear parents ask, "Will Craig learn to mow the lawn?" or "Will Yvonne learn to cook?" or "Will Aloysius learn to wash dishes?" We are more likely to hear, "Will Agnes learn to talk?"

Life can be very difficult when the sounds, gestures, and facial expressions of others make no sense to us and when our attempts to convey thoughts and feelings make no sense to others. For this reason, parents are anxious to have their children learn to understand language and to speak clearly.

For the purposes of this chapter, we shall use *language* to signify the meaningful use of words and *speech* to refer to the mechanics of pronouncing words.

It is possible to have good speech without language comprehension. A child who says words perfectly but without comprehension is no better off than one who cannot speak. When Timmy was found after he had wandered away, a teacher asked him, "Where have you been?" Timmy replied, "I've been to London to visit the queen." Though perfectly spoken, his answer was merely the recitation of a line from a nursey rhyme and meant nothing to him. As for the teacher, she had no better idea of where Timmy had been than if he had said, "Glub, glub."

The music specialist's main contribution toward developing the ability to communicate will be in making the spoken word meaningful. All the song ideas in other parts of this book can help in developing language abilities, although they are used to illustrate other purposes. A few new ideas are given here with suggestions on how to use previously presented material as helps in language development.

The verb song was mentioned before as a simple way of learning the meaning of a verb. The child comes to understand what *walk*, *jump*, or *run* means if he sings or hears the word as he performs the action it represents.

The noun song is most effective when the object named can be seen and handled while it is being sung about.

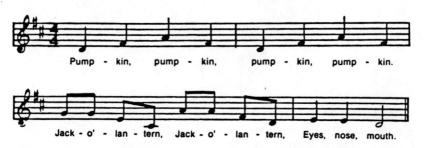

Pump - kin, pump - kin, pump - kin, pump - kin.

Jack - o' - lan - tern, Jack - o' - lan - tern, Eyes, nose, mouth.

The above song requires a pumpkin and a jack-o'-lantern. The child puts his hand on the pumpkin during the first half of the song. He then moves to the jack-o'-lantern, puts his hand on it, and points to its eyes, nose, and mouth when those words are sung.

When words are put to music, accent and differences in pitch can help to emphasize certain words or syllables:

Where is your foot?

"Foot" is emphasized by the change in pitch and by the accent. The teacher could sing this to a child and teach him to point to his foot in response. When the child has learned to do this, the teacher could ask about other body parts and have the child point to them.

The child begins to see, after awhile, that the emphasized word is the one that changes and identifies the part to be located. He also realizes that "Where is your" means that he is to locate something.

The words can later be changed to "Where is the _____?" and known objects anywhere in the room can be chosen as things to be pointed out.

No more than one new word or phrase should be introduced in a song. Children can hear a new word among familiar words, but they cannot identify the new word we want them to learn if it is buried among many unknown words.

The words used in songs must be the same ones used in the classroom. If the teacher is using "middle," the music specialist should not use "center." Or, if the teacher is teaching the class to put something "behind" something else, the specialist must not use "in back of."

Songs can also be used to teach correct usage of words. A child who always says, "Me go home," or "Me eat lunch," may finally learn to say, "I go home," or "I eat lunch," if he sings them long enough and often enough.

While the teacher can help a child develop his understanding of language, he may not be able to do much toward improving a child's speech. Unless the teacher is also a speech specialist, he will find it helpful to ask and follow the speech therapist's diagnoses and recommendations for the group and for individual children. He can then prepare musical material suitable for his group.

The teacher of a group of babblers can set the children's spontaneously spoken syllables to music. Any simple tune with an even rhythm that can be sung slowly is good for this purpose.

People who can talk may also learn to make sounds correctly by singing them. Young children enjoy singing syllables even though they can say some words. Older children, however, should have something less childish to sing, if at all possible. An older boy who talks about crossing the "strit" may not be pleased at being asked to sing, "Street, street, street." Even if he does it, the result will very likely be "Strit, strit, strit," and we must never furnish opportunities for children to practice and perfect their mistakes. What to do? First of all, the problem is to get the child to lengthen the *ee* sound; therefore, the song will have to provide a nice long note on that sound. Since the last note of a phrase is usually long, we shall put "street" at the end of the phrase:

I   look to   the  left,  I   look  to   the right, Be-fore I  cross the   street.

"Street" is on a long note. But our boy will sing "strit" and leave the pianist and other singers to hold the note. So, we shall break our rule, which calls for one note to one syllable, and give "street" two notes:

I look to the left, I look to the right, Be-fore I cross the stree - eet.

In order to sing the second note, our singer will have to hold the first one for three counts. The teacher may still have to exaggerate the way he says the word to keep the child from singing "stri - it."

Let us point out again that these musical devices are meant to ease learning. They are not expected to solve every problem. There is no guarantee that everything we try will help. The examples given worked for our children but the reader may find a child for whom the method does not work. Do not worry. Just try something else.

Children who run syllables together can sometimes enunciate each one clearly if a song separates the syllables by using a different note on each one:

but - ter - fly

If a scale line progression is not easily heard by a child, a chord line with its skips may be better for him:

but - ter - fly

Having all three, or even two of the three, syllables on the same note would allow the word to be sung as it was originally spoken — "buf-fly." There would be no point, of course, in trying this with a child who is unable to say each of the sounds.

Occasionally, a child accents the wrong syllable in a word. This often happens when an adult corrects a child's pronunciation of a word. If Jimmy says he wants "budda" on his bread, and Mother in her desire to help him says, "ButTER," Jimmy may obediently say, "ButTER." Mothers are not the only persons who do this kind of teaching. Teachers can do it too. A boy who said "mewsis" for "music" was told by his teacher that the word was "muZIK." The boy learned to say "muZIK" so well that it became necessary to help him shift the accent. The teacher did this by having him sing the word up the scale.

Mu - sic,    mu - sic,    mu - sic,    mu - sic,

A three-count rhythm was used because it naturally places the accent on the first syllable. The boy quickly caught on and began saying the word correctly.

For short words, singing up or down the scale works very well. Longer words can be made easier by variations in pitch:

I - ma - gi - na-tion,    I - ma - gi - na-tion,    I - ma - gi - na-tion.

The accented syllable falls not only on the strong beat in each measure but on a high note, which helps to emphasize it. Though they will not be using many five-syllable words, even children with limited speech may have to learn a few long words. Kenji Kamibayashiyama, for example, who lives on Beverly Glen Parkway probably could use some musical assistance in learning to give his name and address. If he still cannot learn to do it, perhaps his family will have to change their name to Ito and move to Dee Street.

A good song follows the natural rhythm of the words and is good practice for rhythmic speech. The teacher must therefore make sure that the words to every song he uses are rhythmically correct and that they are sung slowly enough for the children to get the words in. Children with extremely slow speech may need separate turns so that they can sing at their own slow rates.

Children who speak more slowly than necessary may be helped by singing at a slightly faster tempo. Earl was a postencephalitic boy who spoke slowly and unrhythmically because he opened his mouth as far as it would open on each syllable. When the teacher played songs a little faster than Earl would sing them by himself, the boy did not open his mouth all the way because he had to hurry to keep up with the music.

Some children with unrhythmic speech do have good bodily rhythm. Letting these children put themselves into motion before beginning to talk can help them speak more clearly. They can sing or just say the words of a song rhythmically while they sway or walk. Because children do this best when moving at their own tempos, individual turns are necessary for good results.

The teacher and the music specialist will have to keep this kind of work from becoming a speech drill. If the children are annoyed because their manner of speaking is being corrected, we are doing a poor job and would do better to drop the whole thing. But as long as the children are able to enjoy the songs, the teacher and the music specialist can feel safe in continuing the use of songs for speech practice.

*Chapter 11*

# RHYTHM INSTRUMENTS

OF all the things they do in music, children seem to like playing instruments best. The retardate, as we know, has few opportunities for enjoying the pleasures of accomplishment. Rhythm instruments give him that pleasure by letting him bring forth interesting sounds when he shakes them, hits them, blows them, or rubs them together. He can make them boom or crash or jingle. He can make sounds loud or soft, fast or slow; he can make them stop altogether. Our contribution to his enjoyment will be to help him play as well as possible and give him the kind of music that makes his performance sound even better. Instead of emphasizing correctness in his playing, we will try to find the easiest way for him to use the instruments effectively.

SLEIGH BELLS. Sleigh bells are not just easy to play; they are actually hard not to play as they jingle and jangle at the slightest movement. Because of this, bells attached to a cloth loop are good for indiscriminate sound-making as when they are worn on the wrists or ankles while running or dancing. For organized music, bells on a plastic or leather strip attached to a metal handle are better because they are more easily controlled and can be silenced when covered with one hand. Since the bells ring so easily, they are an excellent starting instrument for the child who is unsure of himself and is afraid to try anything new. On the other hand, a hyperactive child will cause the bells to produce a constant jangling because he simply cannot stay still. He should have the opportunity of playing the bells, but for rhythm band or any other structured music activity, he needs an instrument requiring less control. Placing the bells on the floor or on a table or stool until it is time to play can help a very active child. The bells can be played with a more precise beat if they are hit against the palm of the other hand.

RATTLES. Perhaps the most commonly used rattles are maracas— rattles made of gourds. These are colorful and have a nice sound. The gourds will remain solidly on their handles for a longer time if they are reinforced before they are ever used. Wind a string around the handle right at the point where it meets the rattle. Then cover the string with glue and let the glue harden.

Some maracas are too big and clumsy for little hands, so the teacher will have to choose the right size rattles when buying them. They do not have to be big for big people, but they should be small for small people. Plastic maracas are small and light, but they break very easily.

The simplest homemade rattles are made of small tins such as containers of throat lozenges. These may be filled with rice, beans, pebbles, nails, or buttons and taped around the edges. Spraying a coat of paint on the tins will make them look more attractive and less like advertising.

Plastic bottles are also easy to make into rattles. They have a different sound from the ones made of metal even when the same fillers are used. A drop of glue on the threaded mouth of the bottle will help hold the cap in place when it is screwed on. Plastic tape wrapped tightly around the cap and part of the bottleneck will make removal of the cap more difficult. Large bottles may be used if they are shaped so that they are easily held in one hand. These larger rattles can have larger pieces as fillers, but they should not be too large or too heavy to shake with ease.

Small cans with plastic lids may have holes made in top and bottom. A dowel can then be inserted to form a handle. A string wound around the dowel at the top and bottom of the can and well coated with glue will keep the rattle in place. These, too, may be filled with anything that makes a good sound. The handle should be only long enough to fit a child's hand, as too long a handle makes the rattle top-heavy and also encourages its use as a hammer with which to hit floor, walls, furniture, and people.

We suggest making some rattles that look alike but sound different. Then, they can be chosen by sound to fit the music being played. If at least two or three rattles of the same kind (rice, beans, stones, etc.) are made, they can be used for sound discrimination activities such as finding two rattles that sound alike. Be sure that all rattles used for this purpose are similar in weight as well as in appearance.

A child who has difficulty shaking a rattle will sometimes do better with a rattle in each hand. If this does not help, he may be shown how to hit a rattle against the palm of his other hand.

DRUM. In any shape or size, drums are among the most popular instruments. Many children like the little drums (they look like tambourines) with wooden handles. These are held by the handle and struck against the other hand. The motion is similar to hand-clapping and is easy for most children. The handle must be screwed on tightly to keep the drum from turning.

The tom-tom is good for children who like to sit on the floor and beat the drum with two hands. Younger retardates, especially those with poor body images, should hit the drum with the hands so that they can feel what they are doing. Those with poor muscle control are also better off hitting the drum with their hands, as a drumstick, being an extension of the arm, can only be controlled if the arm and hand are controlled.

The snare drum has a rim that gets in the way of some drummers, and it may be necessary to have these children use a stick with a larger knob so that they can avoid hitting the rim. Or it may help to place the drum low enough so that the drummer's hand is too high to allow him to hit the rim while hitting the drumhead.

Bongos are interesting because of the difference in tone. They may be hit with a xylophone hammer if the child cannot get a tone by using his hands.

Larger drums, of course, are easier to hit with sticks than small drums. If our drummer keeps hitting the edge of the drum with the side of the drumstick, he may be able to take better aim if we stick a piece of colored tape in the middle of the drumhead. The drum will also have to be placed at a height and angle that allows for any physical problems a child may have.

String or leather handles may be removed from smaller drums when there are girls or boys who like to swing the drums through the air.

WOOD BLOCK. The wood block may be held in one hand or placed on a table and struck with a drumstick. It is better than the tone block, which is a hollow, cylindrical piece of wood with a handle, as children often become more interested in fitting the striker into the hole in the block than in playing the instrument. The wood block may be fastened to a table or a stand if there is a problem with children who do not use it correctly.

RHYTHM STICKS. The rhythm sticks we purchase for rhythm band work are sometimes unwieldy because they are too long. Make sure that the sticks are not too long and that they have a good tone. Bamboo chopsticks (the large ones that do not come to a point) have a nice clacking sound.

Little children often enjoy hitting the floor with their sticks. These children should be allowed to hit the floor, but they should also be encouraged to hit the sticks together. Children who can hear the difference in sounds made by sticks hitting the floor and by sticks struck together can, if they have the physical coordination and rhythmic feel for it, alternate hitting the floor with the sticks and hitting stick against stick. They may get the idea better if we say, "Floor, stick. Floor, stick," or "Floor, stick, stick. Floor, stick, stick."

If this is too hard, the children may be taught to strike the floor when they have one stick and to hit the sticks together when they have two.

JINGLE CLOGS. The kind of jingle clogs made of one flat piece of wood with jingles nailed or screwed on are easier to use than those with a cone-shaped head into which a handle is set. The flat ones do not turn over, and they cannot come apart. If the sticks are hard to hold, the handle end may be made narrower by sawing off a piece along each side. The handle can then be sanded smooth.

TRIANGLE. A triangle that hangs from one string is easily set to spinning and swinging by the uncontrolled swipes of some children. Once it is in motion, it is hard to hit. Also, some people like to just sit and watch it spin. Instead of letting the triangle hang by one string, we can place a string loop at each of its two closed angles and attach the loops to hooks on the sides of a wooden frame so that the triangle hangs with its open angle down. The horizontal bar at the top will then be steady enough for most children to hit. The shorter the loops, the less swinging there will be.

SANDBLOCKS. The knobs on some sandblocks are so small that they must be held with the fingertips. The handles should be large enough to be grasped easily, but not so large as to be clumsy. Actually, handles are not necessary at all if the blocks are a size that fit the children's hands comfortably. Handles like those on double-hung windows work nicely if they are the right size.

Sandpaper mittens can be made by sewing or stapling together sandpaper and heavy brown paper cut out in the shape of mittens. The rough side of the sandpaper goes on the outside of the palms, and the brown paper fits the back of the hands. The children can hear and feel the effect as they rub their hands together. Emery cloth will last longer than sandpaper.

The sandpapered surfaces of these instruments are supposed to be swished against each other, but some children like to clap them together instead. In order to satisfy those who want to clap, but also to get them to swish, we provide music for both techniques.

CYMBALS. Handles for cymbals are often too small to be held without bracing the hand against the metal disk and should be replaced with larger ones if possible. A strap is satisfactory when the cymbal is to be suspended and struck with a drumstick. Tapping one cymbal with the edge of another gives a lighter sound. If this is too hard to do, the cymbal may be tapped with a light, thin stick. Cymbals can be held down flat on the lap or against the sides to keep them quiet until time to play.

Some children hold the cymbals so far apart that they cannot bring them together in time to play. If explaining the problem to a child does not help, we may have to confine the movement of his arms to a reasonable distance by using our own hands and arms as barriers. Those who can manage it may use the up and down slicing motion in playing the cymbals.

TAMBOURINES. The tambourine is to be grasped with the fingers on the inside and the thumb over the other edge if possible. Some children hold it in one hand and hit it with the preferred hand. This may necessitate the shifting of the tambourine to the preferred hand when it is to be shaken instead of being hit. If it is held in the preferred hand, it can be struck against the heel of the other hand, and it should not be necessary to shift hands in order to shake the instrument. If it is too hard to hold, the tambourine may be placed on the lap, or it can be put on the floor or table and hit with a drumstick. Holding it with one or both hands and hitting the knee is another possibility. There are also children who like to strike the tambourine against their legs while galloping around the room. If the tambourine is too hard to play, jingle clogs made with three or four sets of jingles will give somewhat the same effect.

Shaking the tambourine requires a wrist motion and is not easy for little children. Many younger children can only pump their hands slowly up and down with no action in their wrists. Much of the problem may be that the instrument is too big and heavy for little hands. Tambourines made of paper or plastic plates and bottle-cap jingles are easier to shake. They will have to be handled with care, however, as paper plates may tear, and plastic plates may crack if stepped or sat upon.

HORNS. For the sake of simplicity, we are classifying all toy wind instruments—clarinets, trumpets, saxophones—as horns. Children who are able to say the names of the instruments can be taught to identify them by sight and by their correct names. However, we are talking about inexpensive toy instruments, and it must be remembered that these do not sound or function like the real instruments.

The most simply constructed horns are the ones with holes that have to be covered by the fingers. These are the most difficult for our children to play. To make things easier, we can cover each of the holes with tape, and the children will only need to blow. When a different tone is wanted, we remove the pieces of tape that will expose the holes necessary to give us the desired note. Since the same note will be sounded throughout one song, we can either play the piano in a key that fits the horn note, or we can find the note on the horn that fits in with the piano music.

Some toy horns have keys consisting of a part that covers the holes, and levers or buttons to hold down with the fingers. These horns are easier to play because the player does not have to cover the holes with his fingers; he merely has to press a key and blow. When it does not matter what note is played (as in a Halloween parade), the children can press any key they want to press. But when a note that harmonizes with the music is required, the players will have to use one particular button.

There are a number of ways to get a child to press the right button so that the note sounded will fit in with the music. The simplest way is to show him the right one. It might be the one at the top or the bottom, or it might be the second from the top, or some other one.

There is no problem if a child can hold down the right key after such a simple explanation. However, some children will need more help. We can identify the right key by sticking some bright colored tape on it. Some horns have keys of different colors, and a child who knows colors can be told that he is to use the yellow key or the blue key.

If a child insists upon pushing down lots of different levers because real musicians play that way, we may have to make it impossible for him to sound the wrong note. This can be done by breaking off the pads that cover the holes. The buttons or levers will still move as before. All the holes except the one we need are now covered with tape. The child may then hold down any lever he likes, but only one tone will sound when he blows.

Horns blend nicely into simple music that requires only two basic chords if we play one tone common to both chords:

do   re   mi   fa   sol   la   ti   do

The fifth degree of the scale (sol) will fit in with both chords. In the following example, the trumpet, by playing "A" on all the "toot, toot, toots," will be in harmony with the D and A chords that accompany the song. The trumpet player will either be holding down the button that makes the horn play "A," or he will simply be blowing a horn that has been fixed to play "A" and nothing else.

Blow the trum - pet, blow the trum - pet. Toot, toot, toot.

Blow the trum - pet, blow the trum - pet. Toot, toot, toot.

Blow the trum - pet, blow the trum - pet. Toot, toot, toot.

Blow the trum - pet, blow the trum - pet. Toot, toot, toot.

Children who have the ability to change from one note to another at the right time will enjoy doing so. The teacher only needs to see that the changes do not come too frequently. Each of the buttons to be used can have a different color taped on it. The teacher can call out the color to be played next. Some children may be able to manage several different notes.

Toy horns have an unfortunate habit of changing pitch from time to time, and it is not always possible to have all the children playing the same note. It is a good idea to sound the horn first to determine what key the piano should play in. Purchasing enough horns so that each member of the group can have one eliminates the problem of cleaning the horns during class.

The horns will hold together longer if plastic tape is used to bind them around the bottom and also near the top. The tape can be stretched to fit smoothly so that it is hardly noticeable. Do not tape the mouthpiece.

CASTANETS AND FINGER CYMBALS. The teacher needs to study each child's hand and finger coordination and figure out the best way for him to work these instruments, which are difficult for many children. The finger cymbals may be held in the fingers of each hand and struck lightly together.

TUNED BELLS. The bells we are talking about are those metal bars mounted on wooden blocks and placed in a case so that they can be played like a xylophone. They are easier to use than xylophones or song bells because each bar can be removed from the case and used by itself, making it impossible to hit the wrong note. Even if more than one bell is used, they can be placed far enough apart so that the wrong note is not accidentally played.

Crayons can be used to mark the bells in colors that the children know. All the bells of one color should harmonize. The children play when the teacher calls their colors. Some boys and girls are able to have two or more bells of different colors and play them at the right time.

If we give a child a set of bells that makes up a five-tone scale, he can make music that sounds good no matter what notes he hits. Four easy five-tone scales to pick out are these: all the "black" keys; C,D,E,G,A; F,G,A,C,D; G,A,B,D,E.

AUTOHARP. Many young retarded children are unable to hold down the autoharp bars hard enough to get a clean chord. The teacher can press down the bars for these children, while holding the instrument in the position that makes strumming most comfortable for each child. Some of our children have more success with the autoharp if they can strum down across the strings; this means that the teacher will have to stand the instrument on its edge with the strings running horizontally, the bass strings at the top. Anything that makes playing possible for a child makes a good pick—pencils, erasers, clothespins, sticks.

PSALTERY. The psaltery is a stringed instrument upon which melodies can be played by picking the strings. It is a good instrument for children who like to experiment with tunes.

ORGAN. A small organ is useful for playing chord backgrounds or accompaniments. The keys that make up a chord can have one color of tape on them, and those that make up other chords can have other colors. Depending upon the size of the organ, two or more children can hold down keys as the teacher calls out the colors. Since the organ tone is sustained as long as a key is held down, the children can hold one chord for as long as it needs to be held. Numerals or letters written on tape or on the keys may be used instead of colors.

OTHERS. Anything that makes an interesting sound becomes a musical instrument. Old door chimes, frying pans, pot lids, plastic bottles, novelty toys that moo, tweet, or meow, and bicycle bells and horns are examples of things that can be used. Hardware stores, dime stores, and junk dealers have many items that can be converted into musical instruments.

Some time can be saved and confusion avoided by handing instruments to the children in such a way that they can be taken and held correctly. A pair of cymbals, for example, can be held upright with their flat surfaces together and the edges toward the child so that he naturally reaches for the handles, or drumsticks can be handed out before the drums are distributed so that the child will take it in the hand that will probably do the beating. However, some children grasp the stick with one hand and then shift it to the other. If the teacher is not sure of the child's handedness, he might step back suddenly and wave "Hi!" to the child. The child who is suddenly greeted in this fashion often responds immediately by waving his hand. The teacher may then place the drumstick or tambourine or jingle clog in that hand. This is not a sure indication that the child has a preference for that hand, so if he has trouble using that hand, we shall want to have him try the other.

Some instruments are simple enough to be made by the children. Teachers who want ideas on what to make and how to do it can find books of instructions at any library. If the teacher is making the instruments, he is welcome to try anything he wants; but if the children are to make them, the teacher must be careful to choose instruments that the girls and boys can really make. If the adult does most of the work, the children may feel that the product is not their own, or they may think they have made something wonderful when they really had little to do with it. In either case, the class will have learned little.

Tuned water glasses and pop bottles are fun, but they should be used only with children who can treat them gently; otherwise, there is the danger of shattered glass. It is also hard to keep the glasses in tune if the water is constantly being spilled or imbibed.

## THE RHYTHM BAND

Every child needs the experience of playing all types of instruments for muscle coordination and for rhythmic and tonal appreciation, and he should have this experience whether or not he can play rhythmically. The rhythm band, however, is an organized group with definite parts to be played at definite times. This means that each child is given an instrument and part he can play correctly, or at least well enough to blend into the general effect. But while parts are being learned, all members of the group will have the opportunity of playing each of the instruments used in the orchestration.

The simplest method of performance is to have the group start playing when the music starts and stop playing when the music stops. The instruments used may all be the same or of several different kinds.

A little more attention and control is required when the band must wait until an introduction has been played and the teacher gives a verbal signal to begin. For short pieces, the music can be played through once as an introduction. The signal may be any word that gets a good response. "Go" or "Play" can be used. If everyone is playing the same kind of instrument, the leader might say, "Drums," or "Bells," to indicate that they are to play. Some children respond better to "Boom, boom" or "Shake the bells." "Stop" is the best command for stopping. An accompanying gesture like a nod or shake of the head will help the group to follow verbal directions. This is useful because in the end we shall want to drop all spoken commands and substitute visual cues.

Directions may have to be called far in advance for children who are slow to respond. Inattentive ones will need to be called by name before directions are given. Remembering or noticing which children need to be called to attention, which ones respond quickly, which ones respond slowly, and which ones respond very slowly — all while playing the piano and giving cues at the right time — can keep the teacher rather busy. Some teachers may like to have someone else play the piano for the rhythm band period. Taped or phonograph music can be used, but rehearsing particular sections of the music is much simpler with live piano accompaniment. Members of the band may have to be seated according to how much help they need. Easily distracted or inattentive children should be placed near the teacher so that he will not have to shout over the music or make violent gestures to attract their attention. If a rhythm band is going to play for a group of parents or other interested persons, the teacher should feel free to call out necessary cues or instructions.

When they have learned to wait until they receive the signal to play, the band can be taught to hold instruments quietly until the last part of a song. This requires control, and the song should be short.

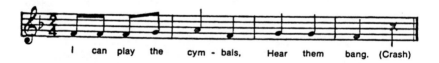

I  can  play  the  cym - bals,  Hear  them  bang. (Crash)

Then, when the children can wait until the end of a song, they can learn to play only when the words tell them to play. In the songs below, the instruments will only play on the "booms" and the "dings."

Hear  my  drum.  Hear  my  drum.  Boom, boom, boom, boom,  boom.

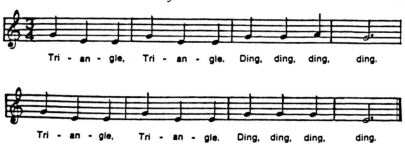

Tri - an - gle, Tri - an - gle. Ding, ding, ding, ding.

Tri - an - gle, Tri - an - gle. Ding, ding, ding, ding.

Music with repetition like the "Triangle" song above is good for practice in playing loud or soft. The first phrase may be played loudly and the second phrase softly, or the first softly and the second loudly. Short songs like the "Drum" song can be played twice, once softly and once loudly.

Next, the class can be divided into three or four sections, each of which plays a different instrument. The teacher starts the first section and, at the proper moment, brings in the second section, then the third, and then the fourth. Each section, once started, continues playing to the end. A short theme repeated with variations that build up in volume is well suited to this kind of cumulative treatment.

Now, instruments can take turns playing:

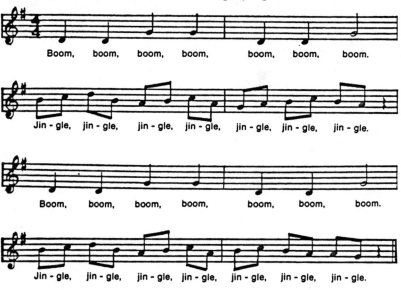

Boom, boom, boom, boom, boom, boom, boom.

Jin - gle, jin - gle, jin - gle, jin - gle, jin - gle, jin - gle, jin - gle.

Boom, boom, boom, boom, boom, boom, boom.

Jin - gle, jin - gle, jin - gle, jin - gle, jin - gle, jin - gle, jin - gle.

The teacher calls out, "Drums" or "Bells," when it is time for them to play. It may be necessary to shake the head or to say, "Stop," before calling the next instrument if some of the first group continue playing. Children who have trouble playing on signal may be able to do better if they sing the words of the song.

Eventually, it becomes possible to use music without words. Older trainables and educables, especially, are better able to hear musical form, and these children can learn to listen for musical cues as well as to look for signals from the teacher.

The assignment of instruments for a rhythm band depends upon the difficulty of the part and the ability of the child. Bells, rattles, sandblocks, rhythm sticks, and jingle clogs can be played by people who do not feel the beat, because bells and rattles can sound all right even if they are shaken without much regard for the beat, while sandblocks, sticks, and jingle clogs can blend into the background if they are not loud. This does not mean that these instruments do not have to be played in rhythm, but that even children who cannot play rhythmically do not have to be left out of the band. Triangles, tambourines, drums, and cymbals can be heard very clearly, and they are better when played by people with good rhythmic sense and muscular control.

Those who can play rhythm patterns can have fun doing so instead of having to pound out the basic beat monotonously. A few retarded children can repeat rhythmic patterns after one hearing, but others need help before they can reproduce the patterns. The help given varies, of course, with the rhythmic design and with the child. Finding the device that proves successful may take some trial and error, but if the part cannot be taught after three or four tries, it probably is too hard and should be simplified or dropped.

Tapping out the rhythm on the child's shoulder or taking his hands and clapping the pattern can be helpful. People who can speak rhythmically are sometimes helped by saying words to the pattern. Angela was unable to play the example below until she said the words first and then played her instrument while she said them again.

Scott,        Scott,        An - ge - la.

The teacher used Scott's name because Angela liked Scott. Whether this was any help to Angela we do not know. But it probably would not have been smart to use the name of someone Angela disliked.

When a rhythm pattern demands silence at certain places, some children may find it helpful to speak while they play as in the following example:

Bang, bang, bang,        Bang, bang, bang.

If a child plays straight through the rest, he may need to tell himself to stop:

Bang, bang, bang, stop.        Bang, bang, bang, stop.

If a child plays straight through even while saying, "Stop," it may be that he is unable to respond quickly enough to his own verbal command. For this child, we may have to change the example so that he has more time in which to react:

Bang, bang, stop.        Bang, bang, stop.

The child will still bang while saying, "Stop," but he may be able to stop on the fourth count. We doubt that a child like this would think that it is right to play on the count when he says, "Stop." It seems more likely that he would associate the word with his action in stopping on the next count.

As songs are easier to learn when they contain repetition, band music with repetition is also easier to learn. In the next example, note the repeated sections.

Norwegian

It is obvious on playing this, that bars 3 and 4, 7 and 8, and 15 and 16 are identical. Let us, then, have the same instrument play the same pattern each time these identical measures are played. We shall have the tambourine play the rhythm pattern given below:

Bars 1 and 2 are the same as bars 5 and 6, while 13 and 14 are a variation of the same thing. Suppose we let the sticks play these parts in a steady rhythm:

Measures 9 and 10 are repeated in 11 and 12. We might let the bells jingle all through these four measures, while the triangle plays on the first count of each:

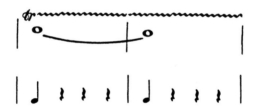

The orchestration is shown on the next page. It can be modified, and other instruments can be added or substituted to make the music as interesting as the children can make it.

What about having a child direct the rhythm band? Some teachers like to have a child stand before the group and wave a stick. Teachers who use a child "director" because it is "cute" are putting on a show instead of training children. One teacher was told that a boy in her class, Eddie, had been the director of the rhythm band in a school he had previously attended. As Eddie had severe physical problems that forced him to stand in a bent-over position and drool constantly, the teacher could not believe that anyone would have exhibited his physical disabilities by letting him lead a band. During the next music class she called the child to the front of the room and

handed him a stick to see if he could really conduct the group. It was evident that the boy was experienced, for he knew what to do, but his movements were so grotesque and, combined with his ecstatic smile, so ludicrous that the adults in the room dissolved into nearly hysterical laughter. Eddie's former teacher had apparently been amused by his efforts and enjoyed entertaining others by having him perform for them. Even if Eddie was not hurt because he was unaware of the reason for the laughter, he was not learning anything or deriving any good from the experience. There is neither time nor reason for cluttering up a training program with activities that do not help the children.

There are some children who can actually direct a group if only one or two kinds of instruments are used. These children may be allowed to conduct the band if the band respects their direction. No matter how well the conductor may be waving his stick and directing sections to play or stop, the band will fall apart unless they follow their leader, or unless they have learned to play by rote in which case a director is unnecessary. If the teacher does the actual directing, it is better not to have a child pretending to conduct, for he would only be a distraction.

If one child is allowed to direct, the others should have turns too. A good time to do this is when an experience unit includes something about a band leader — a unit about a band or a parade, for instance.

## INDIVIDUAL EXPERIMENTATION

Occasionally when a class is small, all the instruments (or a number of them) can be set out where the children can pick up any one they want to play. The teacher may leave them entirely alone, follow the children's lead, and play something that fits in with what they are doing, or help children who seem unsure by playing and encouraging them to join in.

The same can be done with all the drums and no other instrument. The differences in pitch and quality are good for discriminative listening. Interesting rhythmical and tonal effects are sometimes worked out in these sessions. Song bells, psalteries, and other melodic instruments can be experimented with in a similar manner.

## INSTRUMENTS WITH SONGS

Toy instruments can be used to add interest to songs. A triangle or bicycle bell can be rung as an introduction to a song about a telephone; a whistle can be blown in a song about a traffic cop. Old door chimes might accompany a song about answering the doorbell. Shaking a sheet of metal produces a very realistic thunderclap for a song about thunderstorms.

Teachers will find many similar uses for the instruments they have. The children will have ideas to contribute, too, if they are encouraged to think of new things to do with their songs and instruments.

Chapter 12

# GAMES AND DANCES

THE preceding chapters have dealt with ways of putting fun into learning. Now we come to a chapter that purports to turn things around and put learning into fun. These games and dances can help strengthen language comprehension, muscular control, the ability to attend, and the enjoyment of social activity. They have been made as simple as possible so that children with few skills can take part in them. Teachers whose classes are capable of more complicated activities can alter these games and dances or invent some that are suitable for their groups. Those who have children of sufficient physical and mental maturity will be able to use material used by normal children and adults.

## GAMES

Some of these games are merely simplified versions of popular children's games. Wherever possible, words have been chosen to fit the action.

RACES. For the very youngest children, we only want to get across the idea of running to a specified place. The children sit in chairs arranged side by side in a single row. Facing them across the room is a row of empty chairs. When running music is played, the children run across and sit on the empty chairs. At first, the rows of chairs may have to be placed rather close together as there are people who become distracted before they reach their destinations. It is not necessary to play the running music except as a signal to start and as a reminder to some children that they are to run, not stroll.

When they have learned to run from one set of chairs to the other, the class can try something a little more complicated. They begin by sitting in their chairs as before. A box of sleighbells (it can be any small object, but music specialists don't have much to choose from) is placed on a chair or table across the room. As each child's name is called, he runs to the box, picks up a set of bells, and runs back to his chair.

After everyone has had a turn, the procedure is repeated except that the bells are returned to the box instead of being taken from it. To give the runners the idea of starting when a signal is given, the pianist may have the children wait until he says, "Go!" and begins to play.

Now we are ready to begin racing. Two children are told that they are to run. If they can, they wait until they hear "Go!" and the music starts; then they both run and come back with their bells.

The teacher who feels that this is a terribly dull game should remind himself that he is not a retarded four-year-old. Teachers who know children of this level will realize that even something this simple can present difficulties that would make an assistant most welcome. Edwin may decide that this is the perfect opportunity to leave the room. Latonya may run to the box and then run back to her chair without picking up her bells. Ben may run to the table and return with the entire box of bells. Blythe may run to the box and knock everything to the floor with one sweep of her arm.

Perhaps we should stop to consider what measures to take if the conditions just described occur. Doors to the room should be made difficult for Edwin to open so that the teacher has time to see him before he succeeds in escaping. (One good way is to have the doorknob and latch up high where little children cannot reach without standing on a chair. However, this cannot be done in a room where we want children to be able to open and close the door freely.) The teacher can also run along with Edwin when it is his turn, keeping him from straying off toward the door, but not holding him unless it is necessary.

The teacher can also run with Latonya, holding her hand and saying, "Run, run, run," as they go. When they get to the box, he can take Latonya's hand and help her grasp one set of bells and then run back with her. We do not pick up the bells and hand them to the girl because we do not want her to think that she is to run there and wait for someone to hand her something.

When Ben comes back with the whole box of bells, the teacher can walk back to the table with him, have him put the box on the table, and walk back to his chair with him. Now, they start all over. Holding the boy's hand, the teacher runs with him to the table while saying, "Run, run, run," all the way. He helps Ben pick up a set of bells saying at the same time, "Take one." Then, they run, run, run back to Ben's chair. If Ben does not get the idea after a few times (not all in one day), remove the box and leave only one set of bells on the table when it is his turn.

Blythe, also, may need to have only her own bells placed on the table for her so that if she knocks it to the floor she can be asked to pick it up. An adult will have to stay close by to see that she picks up the bells and returns to her chair.

If the table is close enough so that everyone can see what is going on, some children will learn more quickly from seeing what others are doing. The table can be moved farther away when all have learned what to do.

Older children can do the same thing with a slight variation. They are still seated in a row of chairs placed side by side. Two children of comparable ability are chosen to be the first runners. They are not to leave their chairs until everyone has sung the starting signal:

The one who gets back with the bells (or whatever is used) and sits down first is the winner. The reason for having the runners sing is that in their excitement they often do not hear, or cannot wait until they hear, the command to "Go!" when someone else sings it.

At this stage, it is neither necessary nor advisable to mention winning. Later, when children are learning the order of things, they may want to know who was first or second.

Now we can introduce relay racing. In the beginning, it may be difficult to keep the children in their places and keep them from running every time someone else runs. To help maintain order, the participants are seated when they are not running. Chairs may be placed in two rows at one end of the room so that the teams are sitting, facing each other across some five or six feet of space. Because the members of each team are sitting side by side, they can see what is going on better than they could if they were lined up one behind another.

For the time being, this relay will be a series of races between individual representatives from each team. The two persons in the chairs closest to the far side of the room are the first to run. When everyone sings, "On your mark, get set, go!" the two contestants start to run. In order to be sure that the runners go the entire route, they may be required to touch the wall (or a chair or table if there is concern about dirtying the wall) before returning to their chairs. The first to get back and sit down is the winner of that part of the relay, and then each couple runs in turn. Two children of similar abilities should be paired against each other, and the probable winners should be divided equally between the teams if possible.

If the class has some concept of numbers, the winner of each leg of the relay may be given a card to hold until the entire race is over. Then, the children can count the number of people on each team who are holding cards and decide which team has more.

GET THE BALL. This game is very similar to the easy races just described. The children are seated side by side in a row at one end of the room. One child is chosen to be the ball thrower. The thrower stands in the middle of the room with his back to everyone. Two members of the class are chosen to be the runners. When all the players have sung the starting signal, the thrower tosses the ball toward the far end of the room, and the runners try to get the ball. The one who gets the ball is the new thrower.

MUSICAL CHAIRS. This is a version of the familiar game reduced to its lowest terms for very young players. Chairs for each of the children and the teacher are placed in a tight circle facing outward. Everyone walks around the chairs while the teacher and anyone else who can sings:

Walk a - round the chairs. Walk a - round the chairs.

Walk a - round the chairs. Let's sit down.

At the end of the song, everyone sits in a chair.

ALL FALL DOWN. The only words that mean anything to children when they sing, "Ring around a rosy," are "All fall down." Some little children think that any time they join hands in a circle, they are to fall down. This ruins many circle games and dances, so we suggest the following adaptation of a Burmese game as a substitute for "Ring around a rosy."

The children stand one behind another, each with his hands on the shoulders of the child in front. They rock from side to side and then fall down.

Burmese

Rock - ing, rock - ing, rock - ing, rock - ing, Boys and girls.

Rock - ing, rock - ing, rock - ing, rock - ing. All fall down.

Children who cannot wait until the end of the song before falling down can use only the second half of the song. Since they do not often stand behind each other and rock, there is not much danger of the children learning to fall down every time they line up in single file.

FALLING ARCH. London Bridge can be a very messy game for our children; the bridge collapses at the wrong time, the boats go every which way, and the bridge posts get so close together that nothing can get through. Our simplified game should make things easier for both teacher and children. A circle is marked on the floor, and two squares are marked on opposite sides of the track at one point. The two children who stand in the squares face each other and hold hands, forming an arch. The others march around the circle and under the arch until the end of the song when the arch falls down and captures one of the marchers.

American

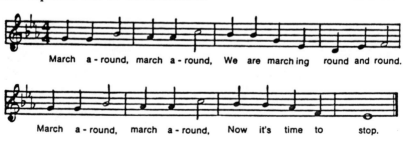

March a - round, march a - round, We are march ing round and round.

March a - round, march a - round, Now it's time to stop.

The captured child replaces one of the two who form the arch, and the one replaced joins the marchers. The circle must not be too large or all the marchers may be on the other side of the circle when the arch falls. Children who have a hard time forming the arch may stand with a hula hoop between them with one edge resting against the floor so that the marchers can walk through the hoop. At the end of the song, the hoop can be pulled away so that the next marcher cannot go through; this marcher will take the place of one of the hoop holders.

EASTER EGG GAME. "It" leaves the room. The Easter Bunny, carrying a basket of eggs, hops around and hides one or more eggs while the others sing:

"It" returns to find the eggs and put them into a basket while the rest of the class sings:

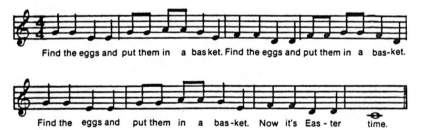

The singers and the pianist can help the hunter by singing and playing more loudly as he gets closer to a hidden egg. This addition to the game should only be made for children who understand that the changes in volume are clues to tell them when they are getting close to their quarry.

BEANBAG ON THE HEAD. The song is as follows:

Margaret's walk-ing with a bean-bag on her head.
(Dwayne is)                                    (his)

Margaret's walk-ing with a bean-bag on her head.

Don't drop it, Mar-garet. Don't drop it, Mar-garet.

Margaret's walk-ing with a bean-bag on her head.

The children sit in a circle. Margaret walks around with a bean-bag balanced on her head. This is not really a game, but the song makes the exercise more interesting than just walking around balancing a beanbag.

For children who have trouble balancing the beanbag, make rather large, flat beanbags with less filling in them. If a beanbag is too easy to balance, use one that is more tightly packed with beans or try some other item that is harder to use.

## DANCES

The kinds of dances done by our trainable retarded children will be determined by the skills already mastered by each child in the group. Physical skills obviously need to be considered, for only movements that can be done by the least physically capable child will allow participation by the entire group. However, if there is only one severely handicapped child in a group of fairly well-coordinated children, we may have to use material too difficult for that child, and we shall have to think of some way in which he can take part. Perhaps he could call out the motions to be made or help form the arch through which other dancers go. It may even be possible to change the dance so that this one member can be given a part to perform.

A child who runs about unable to confine himself to the places and movements required by the dance can spoil the performance for everyone else. Though a teacher may not want to separate a child like this from the group, he may have to do so if the rest of the class is to derive any good from the activity. It may be possible to have that child move around in another area while the others work together. Andre, a boy who was able to do all the gross motor exercises with the other children, could not control himself enough to operate within the prescribed limits of a dance. The music specialist, therefore, had him stay near the piano and the chairs while the rest of the class danced. The specialist spoke to him from time to time so that he would not feel ignored, and the boy jumped, stood on chairs or on the piano bench, or turned in circles as long as the dancing continued. Later, he rejoined the group for work that would not be ruined by his hyperactivity.

Children who do not realize when they are out of position may be able to stay put if they have squares marked on the floor. If they leave the squares, they will know where to go when they are reminded to return to their places.

The dances discussed in this chapter are not the usual folk or square dance. We are not talking about that type of well-rehearsed dancing that almost becomes a habitual response to certain musical pieces. The purpose of our dances is to give children practice in moving to music, attending to verbal direction and musical form, and associating words with action.

By varying the order of calls in longer dances, the teacher can make sure that the children are listening and responding to directions and not moving automatically out of habit. Since some children take longer to grasp directions and respond to them than do others, the total effect of the dance may be somewhat ragged if we change the order of the calls, but our dancers will get more value from the exercise than they would if they always did it the same way.

The children may sing with these dances if they wish, but for clarity and preciseness, the teacher should speak the words instead of singing them.

Dances for the very youngest children may not seem like dances at all because of their simplicity. They should be done in one spot and not include walking or running or other motions that move them away from their starting positions, because it is easier for teachers to help them if they stay together.

Jump.   Jump.   Jump.   Jump.   Turn  a - round.

Stamp, stamp, stamp. Stamp, stamp, stamp.  Clap, clap, clap, clap,  bow.

The next dance is done by partners who face each other and do just what the words say.

Old Song

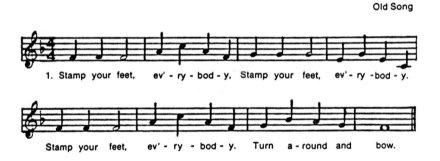

1. Stamp your feet,   ev' - ry - bod - y,  Stamp your  feet,   ev' - ry -bod - y.

Stamp your  feet,   ev' - ry - bod - y.  Turn  a - round  and   bow.

   2. Jump, jump, everybody.
   3. Sway, sway, everybody.
   4. Tap your partner, everybody. (Tap shoulders.)
   5. Swing your partner, everybody. (Lock elbows
      or hold both hands of partner.)

For the following dance, the children stand on a circular track, all facing the same way so they can walk around the track. If a group is composed of people who move at different tempos, the children can take turns performing as couples to avoid the bunching or bumping that results when people move around at different speeds in a confined area.

Danish

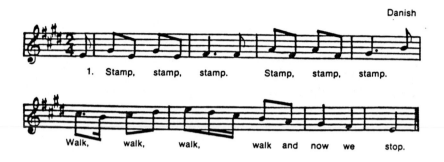

1. Stamp, stamp, stamp. Stamp, stamp, stamp.

Walk, walk, walk, walk and now we stop.

2. Clap, clap, clap.
3. Jump, jump, jump.

Dances that require the participants to take hands, drop them, and take them again are harder to do. For children who are able to do this, we use dances like the following. The dancers stand in a circle, only holding hands when they slide.

Swedish

1. Up, down, Clap, clap, clap. Up, down. Clap, clap, clap.

Slide, slide, slide, stop. Turn a - round and clap, clap, clap.

1. Rise on toes, then down.
2. Stamp, stamp. Clap, clap, clap.
3. Step, step. Clap, clap, clap. (Step forward.)
   Back, back. Clap, clap, clap. (Step back.)
4. Heel, toe. Clap, clap, clap.

Simple dances may have more complicated movements added, and difficult dances may be simplified. Many music books for children contain dances that can either be used as given or adapted for use with retarded children of various levels.

A few sample dances are presented on the following pages. They may be changed in any way that makes them more useful. In a group that is unable to perform together, some of these dances can be done by one child or by one couple while the rest of the class watches, sings, claps, or plays instruments. The bow is a simple bending from the waist.

Moving to the center of a circle is hard for some children, so we can use some tactics that may be helpful. We can draw several diameters through the circle so that our circle looks like a wheel with spokes. As the children stand on the edge of the circle, the converging lines seem to help draw them toward the center.

Some children take long steps and bump people coming in from other parts of the circle. This sometimes becomes such fun that everyone tries to achieve a smashup, and no one returns to the perimeter of the circle to continue the dance. To avoid this, a small circle can be drawn inside the large one, and the children can be shown how to stop when they reach the inner circle (Figure 2).

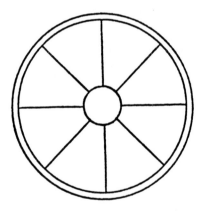

Figure 2

I

Lithuanian

Hold hands in a circle, facing center.

I. Measures 1-4. Walk around.
              5 and 6. Clap.
              7 and 8. Turn around.
              9 and 10. Clap.
              11 and 12. Turn around.

II. Measures 1-4. Walk around.
              5 and 6. Stamp.
              7 and 8. Turn around.
              9 and 10. Stamp.
              11 and 12. Turn around.

The teacher can just say, "Walk," for the first measure, or "Walk, walk," for each measure. In either case, it is probably best to say, "Stop," on Measure 4 so that the children will be ready to clap on Measure 5.

# II

Polish

Stand in a circle, facing center. Measures 9 through 16 are done the same way throughout the dance.

I.   Measures 1-8. Rise on toes one measure, down on next.
       9-12. Hold hands and walk around.
       13-16. Walk in opposite direction.

II.  Turn around on first measure; clap hands on next. Continue through Measure 8.

III. Hands at waist, bend to left on Measure 1; stand erect, Measure 2; bend to right, Measure 3; stand, Measure 4.

IV.  Turn head to one side, first measure; face front, second measure. Turn head to other side, third measure; face front, fourth measure. Repeat.

V.   Bend forward, first measure; stand erect, second measure.

VI.  Squat, first measure; stand, second measure. If this is too hard, squat on first measure, rise on third.

# III

Danish

Children stand in two lines facing each other. Each dancer takes both hands of the person directly opposite.

Measures 1-4.   (Repeated.) Swing arms from side to side.

        5-12. All couples except the last in line raise their hands, still clasped, and form an arch. Last couple walks through and takes its place as the head couple.

If the children cannot form an arch big enough for a couple to pass through, they can hold two sticks between them instead of holding hands. This will enable them to stand farther apart and make a bigger passageway.

Children stand in two lines about four feet apart, facing each other. To keep the lines apart and partners facing each other, squares can be taped on the floor for the dancers to stand on.

I.   Measures 1 and 2. One line walk forward, stopping before they run into their partners.
     3 and 4. Walk back.
     5 and 6. Forward.
     7 and 8. Back.

II.  Measures 1 and 2. Second line walk forward.
     3 and 4. Back.
     5 and 6. Forward.
     7 and 8. Back.

III. Measures 1 and 2. Change places with partner opposite.
     3 and 4. Return to position.
     5 and 6. Change with partner.
     7 and 8. Return to position.

IV.  First line makes 90-degree turn so that children are standing one behind the other. The first child in line leads them in a march behind the other line of dancers and back to their own squares.

V.   Second line walk around first line and back to place.

VI.  Take partner's hands and swing each other around.

## V

Hungarian

Stand one behind another in a circle (not too close together).

Measures 1 and 2. Walk.

        3 and 4. Jump.

        5 and 6. Walk.

        7 and 8. Jump.

Repeat first eight measures.

Measures 9-12.  Step sideways toward center.

        13-16. Step sideways back to position.

Repeat measures 9-16.

If the circle is too small, children can move away from the center in bars 9 through 12 and return to place on bars 13 through 16.

# VI

Creole

Stand in a circle, facing center, holding hands.

I.    Slide in a circle.

II.    Measures 1 and 2. Raise right knee; lower right knee.

             3 and 4. Raise left knee; lower left knee.

             5-8. Repeat measures 1-4.

(If this is too hard, use only one knee. After sliding in a circle, do it with the other knee.)

III.   Slide in a circle.

IV.   Squat, one measure; stand on next. (If necessary, two measures may be used to get down and two to get up.)

V.    Slide in a circle.

VI.   Raise arms on one measure; lower them on the next.

VII. Slide in a circle.

# VII

American

Stand in a circle, holding hands.

Measures 1 and 2. Walk to center.

        3 and 4. Walk back.

        5 and 6. Walk to center.

        7 and 8. Walk back.

        9-12. Slide in a circle.

        13-16. Slide in other direction.

Repeat measures 1-8.

## VIII

Dutch

Couples in a circle, facing forward, ready to move counterclockwise.

Measures 1-8. Run, holding partner's hand.

         9 and 10.  Bow to partner, then clap.

        11 and 12. Bow to partner, then clap.

        13 and 14. Stamp.

        15 and 16. Turn around, take partner's hand, and be ready to repeat the dance.

Chapter 13

# MUSIC AND EDUCABLE CHILDREN

CHILDREN cannot be grouped effectively purely on a basis of similarity in an isolated trait such as mental age, for there are many other factors to be taken into account, such as chronological age, personality, emotional and social maturity, cultural background, experiential background, physical size and development, language development, speech, and medical history. Since people do not develop and acquire skills evenly in all areas, we see trainable children who are further advanced in some ways than educable children of the same chronological age, and educable children who, in some respects, trail behind children of lesser ability. For this reason, it is necessary to consider how the children function overall, both as individuals and as members of a group. We may find a child, for instance, who works well with children of higher mentality than his own because he is socially mature enough to fit in with them. On the other hand, we may find an educable child whose indulgent parents have prevented him from learning some of the basic self-help skills that trainable children are expected to master.

There are no lines to separate low trainables from middle trainables and middle trainables from high trainables, and there is no point that marks the end of the trainable category and the beginning of the educable. The designations of *trainable* and *educable* are made by arbitrarily drawing a line at a point usually determined by an IQ. Schools often look upon trainables and educables as two different kinds of people.

Actually, the same kind of thinking that planned programs for trainable retarded children is operable in setting up programs for educable children. The teacher still plans the classroom program after assessing the achievements and abilities of the group. The music specialist still organizes a music program based on the classroom goals. Just as some musical activities appear in trainable programs at several different levels, so will some activities be included in both trainable and educable programs. There are no musical activities that are expressly for trainables or for educables.

133

We have stated that teachers of educable classes may have to extend the ideas presented in earlier chapters. Some teachers will have to modify those given here as well. Teachers of trainable groups can simplify the suggestions we make for educable children if doing so will render them more useful.

## MUSIC AND EMOTIONS

The value of music as an emotional outlet has been discussed previously. Singing, playing instruments, rhythmic exercise, and dancing are effective and acceptable ways for many people, including "perfectly normal" adults, to head off an explosion of pent-up feelings. Since an educable child usually has better speech and language ability and better physical coordination than many trainable children, he is better able to communicate his own feelings through words and through controlled physical movements and various forms of music.

Some children set their thoughts and feelings to familiar tunes, thus giving us an indication of what is going on inside of them. Ellen was a child whose rejecting parents placed her in a residential school when she was very young. To relieve their guilt feelings, the parents overwhelmed their daughter with gifts, and the girl soon learned to equate gifts with love. While she was at home on vacation, Ellen saw how her father was coping with his problems, but she said nothing about it upon her return to school. One day, after the class had sung a song about the Sleeping Beauty who slept until she was awakened by a prince, the teacher let the class act out the story, which ends with a royal wedding. Ellen wanted to extend the story by adding a few original stanzas—"They opened up their presents," "The king got drunk and fell down," and, "They carried him to bed."

At times, a child may find a song that expresses his feelings for him in a very satisfactory way. Joey, who hated his mother and wished her dead, was delighted one evening at camp when a counselor taught the boys a song. For days after that, Joey went around laughing loudly and singing, "Oh, I'm a villain, a dirty, dirty villain; I put poison in my mother's cup of tea."

Sometimes, listening to a musical story accomplishes the same purpose. Joey enjoyed listening to a recording of "Til Eulenspiegel's Merry Pranks." He listened with much excitement, pumping his feet up and down, at times singing along with the record. Til's escapades made him laugh, but his own guilt feelings demanded that Til suffer a penalty for the troubles he caused, and he loudly intoned judgment along with the judge when Til came to trial. Joey's mother, for some reason, had talked with him about souls going to Heaven, and it meant a great deal to Joey that Til's soul, after his execution, floated toward Heaven. The music specialist never pointed out to him that the tones representing Til's soul finally drift downward.

Groups of children sometimes work out dramatizations using songs and instruments to act out what they are thinking and feeling. Here, again, we urge teachers and music specialists to confine their efforts to providing opportunities for beneficial musical experiences and avoid dabbling in amateur psychotherapy.

Instrumental music can be very satisfying for students who need a change from more academic routines. Those who have learned to use a variety of instruments may want to play them either formally under direction or more creatively by improvising. Some children like to relax by sitting at a piano or other instrument and picking out tunes; others enjoy playing an autoharp or ukelele while they sing.

## LANGUAGE AND SPEECH

Much emphasis in an educable curriculum is placed on language because it is important to an individual's happiness that he have language skills, both receptive and expressive. Parents of educable children may become more upset than parents of trainable children when speech is delayed in their offspring, probably because the educable child seems closer to normal and is expected to behave more nearly normal.

Teachers and music specialists will want to consult the speech pathologist to find out about the students' speech problems—the condition, the cause, the type of therapy needed. The musical applications should come after the pathologist has explained what needs to be done with the child. We should not, for example, insist upon having Charlie sing, "Chewy, cherry chocolate chunks. Chomp, chomp, chew, chew, chomp, chomp, chomp," for practice in saying "ch" correctly, if the speech pathologist feels that Charlie, for the present, should be encouraged to express himself verbally and not be pressured to speak correctly.

The use of songs for practice in correcting troublesome speech sounds and for introducing new words has been discussed previously and probably needs no further discussion. Any song that has words in it is a speech song, of course, but it should be sung at a proper tempo for the child, as too fast a tempo will cause words to be run together, while too slow a tempo can result in unrhythmic articulation.

## MUSIC AND TEACHING

The greatest difference between trainable and educable programs is in academic studies. Educable curricula will include more in this area, but there will be some overlapping at the high trainable and low educable levels.

Because many educable children can say words whose meanings they do not understand, the teacher must be careful to see that the songs they sing are really understood. One way to do this is to put off using songs until the concept being taught is thoroughly learned. The singing would then be for reinforcement.

If a song is taught first, it may promote the rote learning of an idea such as "Two and two are four," even though the singers have no understanding of what they are saying. Bruce, a child who had little speech, was playing with small blocks at a table one day, when he said to the teacher, "See?" Putting two blocks on the left, he said, "Two." Putting two other blocks on the right, he said, "Two." Then, pushing all the blocks together, he triumphantly stated, "Four!" If Bruce had been taught to sing, "Two and two are four," before he had discovered this fact, the song would have meant nothing to him. If he were taught the song *after* his discovery, it would have reinforced the learning and would also have taught him to state the fact verbally.

Words for songs may be written on charts, or each child can have his own book of songs written either by the teacher or by the child. If desired, an illustration (drawn, cut out and pasted, or colored) can be placed on the page facing the song.

For songs in which one word is changed for each stanza, the lyrics may be printed on a poster with a space left for the word that is to be changed. Slits are made so that a card with the word to be sung can be slipped into place before each stanza. Scotch tape at the ends and along the edges of each slit will help prevent tearing. An envelope in which to keep the word cards may be glued or taped to the back of the poster.

Children who have not learned to read may use pictures to remind them of the words of a song they are learning. The pictures are placed on a chart in order from top to bottom or from left to right.

## EXPERIENCE UNITS

Experience units for educable children are prepared in the same way that we described earlier. A sample unit is presented here. The unit topic is percussion instruments, and the objectives are to learn to recognize and name several percussion instruments by sight and sound. The activities are merely examples of things that can be done; they were prepared for a school, not a class, so there is a wide range in the difficulty of the tasks. We have neither reduced each activity to its simplest form nor developed it to its greatest complexity.

The instruments chosen for the unit are cymbals, snare drum, bass drum, timpani, claves, sleighbells, triangle, castanets, maraca, wood block, tambourine, and gong. Teachers who try a unit like this should choose instruments on the basis of availability, distinctiveness of tonal quality, and ease of recognition by sight. Other things to consider are how well the children can pronounce the names, and whether they will be able to read the names. Fewer or more instruments can be used as desired.

The introductory activity would be to visit a local high school or college band, or to have a band visit the school. The class may be prepared for the experience by being told to look for instruments that are played by hitting or shaking.

The percussion instruments can be introduced by the band director if he can do it simply enough; otherwise, a teacher may need to explain things to the children. The instruments could be shown and played one at a time and then presented in short passages of band music that illustrate their typical use.

The band presentation can be recorded on tape and edited to remove the explanatory material, leaving the instrumental parts to be used for practice in identifying instruments.

The items below are listed by activity and not by skill because some activities require the use of several skills. Some of these would be placed on an activity table for individuals or small groups to use independently, while others would be used under direction.

PERCUSSION INSTRUMENT PICTURE LOTTO. Take two large cards (about 9″ × 12″) and mark off each of them into twelve squares. Paste a picture of each of the instruments onto the squares on each card. Cut one of the cards into twelve small cards. The child takes the small cards and matches them with the pictures on the large card, placing the small card on the square that has the matching picture. If two 9″ × 12″ cards are used for the game board, each picture can have an empty square under it. The player can then place the matching picture card below the picture on the game board, and it will be possible to see any mistakes that are made.

This may be played as a regular lotto game. The large cards should have only six or nine squares so that no card has all the instruments. Enough small cards will have to be made to equal the number of pictures on the large cards. The caller picks up a card, looks at it, and asks, "Who has the (gong)?" A child who has the picture answers, "I have the (gong)," and puts the little card on his game board. The player who matches all his pictures first is the winner.

PERCUSSION INSTRUMENT PICTURE AND WORD LOTTO. This is done in the same manner as the picture lotto game, except that the printed word is matched with the picture, instead of picture with picture. One set can be made with the pictures on the game board, and another can be made with the words on the game board. When a child plays by himself, he uses small cards that have the name of an instrument on one side and a picture of that instrument on the other. He can then check to see if he has correctly read the word by looking at the picture on the back of the card. When played by more than one person, the words should be on the game boards and the picture on the small cards.

FLASH CARDS. These are picture cards of the instruments, with the name of the instrument printed on the back of each. A child who is learning to read the names of the instruments can practice by holding the cards name side up and checking to see if he has read the names correctly by turning the cards over to look at the pictures.

Two people may use the flash cards together. One holds up a card and shows the word to his partner. He asks, "What is this word?" If the partner gives the correct answer, he gets the card.

If one corner of each card is snipped off (upper right-hand corner, for example), the players can quickly stack the cards for use by making sure that all the snipped corners are in the same position, and they will not have to worry about coming across a card with the answer side up or with the word upside-down.

PERCUSSION INSTRUMENT WHEEL. This is a dial that can be turned to show pictures of the various instruments on one side and the names of the instruments on the other (Figure 3).

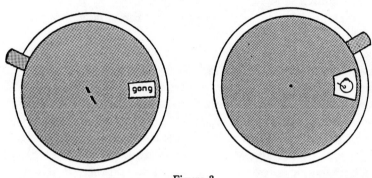

Figure 3

Cut a circle about ten inches in diameter out of heavy cardboard. Mark off the circle into twelve equal wedges. Draw or glue a picture of an instrument about 1¼ inches from the rim of each wedge.

Prepare two circles nine inches in diameter, one with a slot large enough to show one picture at a time when placed over the larger wheel and the other with a slot only large enough to show the printed name of an instrument.

The large wheel is placed between the two smaller wheels. Be sure that the wheel with the picture slot is placed over the picture side of the large wheel. Hold the wheels together with a large paper fastener through the center.

Turn the front circle until the slot is in place right over the picture of an instrument—a snare drum, for example. Turn the entire wheel over, and turn the back circle until the word slot is on the right side, directly across the circle from the picture of the snare drum. Write *snare drum* in the space under the word slot.

Take two 1″ × 4½″ tabs of some stiff material, such as plastic, and glue them together at one end. Round off the corners at that end. When the glue is dry, glue each of the loose ends to the inner surface of the smaller circles about an inch above the picture slot.

This forms a handle that turns the two outer wheels simultaneously while the middle wheel is held still, revealing one picture and one word at a time. After the handle has been attached, turn the wheel to each picture and write its name in the space under the slot on the back of the wheel. The wheel will last longer and stay cleaner if both surfaces of the large circle and the outer surface of each smaller circle are covered with clear adhesive plastic.

A left-handed wheel can be made by placing the picture slot and the word slot on the left side and attaching the handle about an inch above the picture slot.

TWO OF A KIND. Glue pictures of the percussion instruments on cards about 2″ × 3″, one on a card. Since we are working with twelve instruments, there will be twelve cards in a set. Make two sets of cards. Make an additional card that has the picture of a clown or animal or other nonmusical object.

Three or four may play. When the cards have been dealt, the dealer begins by looking at his cards to find two that match. If he finds a pair, he picks out those two cards and lays them down saying, "I have two (castanets)." Even if he has two more matching cards, he keeps them, and play proceeds to the left. When each person has had one turn, the dealer proceeds as in Old Maid, drawing one card from the player on his left and then looking for matching pictures. If he cannot find two alike, he says to the player to his left, "It's your turn," or whatever the teacher decides is the best way for the children to indicate that they have no matching cards and therefore cannot play: "My cards are all different," or "My cards don't match," for example.

The game may be played until all players are rid of cards except the loser, who is sitting with the picture of a clown. If the players are children who become all upset at losing, the game may be ended as soon as one person has finished, and a new game may be started.

For more than four players, two more sets of cards may be used; however, since a game with many players makes long waits between turns necessary, it may be better to have two games going than to have one game with many players.

WHO GETS THE CARD? Use cards of the Two of a Kind game, omitting the clown. Spread out the cards of one set in front of two players. A third child, the caller, uses the other set of cards from which one instrument card has been removed. The caller looks at his first card and says, "Find the (cymbals)," or "Where are the (cymbals)?" The first player to find the correct picture picks it up and says, "I found the (cymbals)," or "Here are the (cymbals)." The players keep the cards they find, and the cards are counted at the end of the game to see who has more. One card will be left over.

PICTURES TO COLOR. Large outline pictures of the instruments are provided so that children can color them with crayons or watercolors or anything else they are learning to use. These may be bound into a book.

PICTURES TO COLOR AND WORDS TO WRITE. The same pictures used for the activity above may be used; however, a line is added under the picture where the pupil can write the name of the instrument. Others may have enough lines for a sentence or short paragraph describing the instrument. If there is not enough room for both picture and writing on the same sheet of paper, they may be done on two separate sheets and made into a book with the pictures facing the written work. If there are objections to the blank pages in such a book, the blank sides may be stapled or rubber cemented together.

PICTURES TO CUT OUT AND PASTE. The kind and amount of cutting depends upon the skill of the cutters. Some may have straight lines or circles drawn on which to cut. Others may cut along the outer perimeter of the instruments themselves. The cutouts can be pasted onto separate sheets of paper or onto one large sheet to make a chart.

WORDS TO CUT OUT AND PASTE. Names of the instruments are printed on a sheet of paper. These are cut out and pasted next to the pictures.

BOOK AND TAPE RECORDING. Under the picture of each instrument, write a short statement about the instrument. Each page ends with, "The (*name of instrument*) says, 'Turn the page.'" The text is recorded on tape, and after each reading of "Turn the page," three tones are played on the instrument just described. Children who cannot read will thus know when to turn the page, and all children will be able to associate the pictures of the instruments with their sounds.

A few examples are given below. The sounds are recorded on tape, but the words in parentheses do not appear in the book.

These are the cymbals. Listen to the cymbals crash. (Crash. Crash.)

The cymbals say, "Turn the page." (Crash, crash, crash.)

This is a tambourine. Listen to it rap and jingle. (Rap, rap, jingle.)

The tambourine says, "Turn the page." (Rap, rap, rap.)

A good way to make a simple book is to use Gamble Hinge Tape to bind the pages. This is a cloth tape that is hinged. It prevents pages from falling apart and allows the book to open flat. The tape comes in rolls of 2-, 3-, 4-, 5-, and 6-leaf sizes. Each size can hold up to twice as many pages as it has leaves. It is also possible to sew two or more tapes together if the book has more than twelve pages. Tape the front cover into place first, then add all the pages and the back cover in order. The hinge can be hidden and the binding strengthened by the addition of wide cloth or plastic tape along the hinged edge, overlapping the covers.*

PUTTING AWAY INSTRUMENTS. A toy book shelf or cabinet is to be filled with instruments. Each player has an individual game board that has been printed on 8½" × 11" paper, backed with cardboard, and covered with clear plastic (Figure 4). The advantage of individual game boards is that no one has to look at the board sideways or upside-down as is necessary when only one large game board is used. The squares on this particular board are counted from left to right in each row. Each player also has a small marker to move around the game board. This can be any little thing that will not roll or fly away. There are twelve small cards, each bearing the picture of one percussion instrument.

Each player picks a card with a picture of the instrument he wants to put away and sets it down by his game board. He also puts his marker on START.

A die may be used to show the players how many squares to move their markers, or the teacher may want to make a spinner that will point to numerals or to number words.

The player who throws or spins the highest number starts the

---

*Gamble Hinge can be obtained from Gamble Music Company, 312 S. Wabash, Chicago, Illinois 60604.

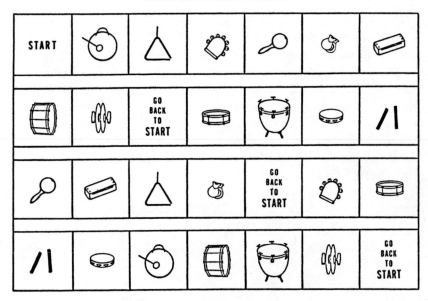

Figure 4

game. Players move their markers by counting the number of spaces determined by a throw of the die or by a turn of the spinner. If the marker stops on a picture of the instrument he has chosen to put away, the player puts his instrument card on a shelf and chooses another instrument to put away. Each square on the board is counted, and a player only goes back to START when his marker stops on a "Go back to START" square. Otherwise, he counts straight through the squares, including the START square.

INSTRUMENTS TO MAKE. Decorate large coffee cans or plastic bottles for drums. Make rattles of small juice cans and dowels. Suspend pan lids for gongs. Make bottle cap and plastic plate tambourines. Stain or paint six-inch lengths of one-inch doweling for claves. Make cymbals by hammering aluminum foil pans flat and screwing on knobs for handles.

TAPE RECORDING. Make a recording that tells the name of an instrument and then follows with sounds from that instrument. Make a second recording that asks, "What is this instrument?", then plays one instrument and gives children time to name the instrument before saying, "That was a (gong)." Make several versions of this tape so that the listeners will not memorize the order in which the instruments are presented.

PLAYING INSTRUMENTS. The instruments are played individually as well as in ensemble. The example given below provides opportunities for all players to play together as well as for individuals or sections to play by themselves. The first two phrases are not repeated once they have been sung and played. The last two phrases are repeated until all the instruments of the band have had their solo opportunities. The teacher should bring in the solo instruments in different order every time the piece is performed so that the players will listen attentively and be ready to play when their instruments are called.

All sing:

This is our band, our per-cussion band. We can play all togeth-er or a - lone.

All instruments:

Teacher:              Claves:              Teacher:              Cymbals:

Listen to the cla-ves.                    Listen to the cymbals.

All instruments:

WHAT DID YOU HEAR? Two identical sets of percussion instruments are placed so that a child who is sitting or standing in front of one set cannot see or be seen by the child at the other set. The children may simply stand with their backs to each other, or they may be screened off from each other by some kind of room divider. One child plays an instrument, and the other child tries to match the sound with an instrument from his own set.

Speech can be added to the game. The first child plays an instrument and asks, "What did you hear?" The other child replies, "I heard a (snare drum)," and plays the instrument.

STORY TAPE. Children make a tape recording telling their own stories of the instruments.

During the entire unit period, the regular classroom work proceeds as usual, except that percussion instruments and information about the instruments are drawn into the work wherever it fits in.

As a final activity for this unit, the class might invite people to a presentation similar to the introductory activity. This time, however, they are the ones who are telling others about percussion instruments. A child can tell about one instrument; then, one child or a group of children can play that instrument with the piano. When this has been done with each instrument, several rhythm band selections can be played as a grand finale.

## Chapter 14

# EXPERIENCE-SHARING PROGRAMS

THIS chapter continues the purpose of all previous chapters — to stress the value of music as a tool in training the retarded. For this reason, there will be no discussion of student performances put on for the entertainment of an audience. The programs discussed in these pages are planned for the children, not for an audience. The classes simply invite someone (other classes, parents) to share their learning experiences. There is some excitement because of the difference in atmosphere — visitors and possibly a change in location — and children are particularly exhilarated by the opportunity to show their families and friends what they do in school. There is no fear of giving a poor performance, for the children know what they are doing. The performance, in fact, is just another review of a learning experience, but one that is even more fun than usual because it is shared by others.

This kind of demonstration is a natural culmination of an experience unit such as the ones referred to in the book. In order to clarify the process involved in presenting this type of program, we shall take a unit from its beginning to the experience-sharing activity.

Let us suppose that we are to have a unit on the circus. First of all, we must decide whether each class will have its own culminating activity or whether several classes will combine their work. Since a circus requires a large number of performers and since we have several groups that work well together, we shall have a circus presented by a combination of these groups.

The teachers of the groups meet together, well in advance of the visit to the circus, and talk over the kinds of learning activities that will probably be used. If the music specialist is present, he will take note of these so that he can begin preparing songs and rhythm exercises to be used with the activities. Between this time and the introduction of the new unit, the teachers prepare lessons and get together the materials they are going to need for their respective classes.

The introductory activity is attendance at a real circus performance. The teachers try to make sure that their classes see all the acts and tell them what the different performers and animals are.

In the days that follow, class activities are built around the circus theme. The activities differ from group to group because abilities differ from group to group. Simple costumes and other properties are made, using skills the children have learned.

The music specialist teaches songs and has the children do rhythm exercises such as galloping or raising the knees high while walking (horses), walking the balance beam (tightrope walker), walking slowly while swaying (elephants), jumping and doing somersaults (acrobats), or rolling on the floor (lions). He also has them play rhythm band music.

When several days have passed, the material produced is put to use as it is completed. Things the children have cut or painted are mounted on large sheets of paper and used as posters. Costumes may be worn and other equipment used when children are imitating the acts they saw.

Toward the end of the unit period, the teachers and music specialist meet again to plan the final activity. During the weeks of the circus unit, the children have had opportunities to play all the parts, but for the program we shall have to limit each child to one or two parts.

First, we shall list the people and animals that will be needed for our circus: acrobats, band, clowns, dogs, elephants, horses, lions and lion tamer, ringmaster, and vendors.

The teachers must now decide in what way each child will participate. Many factors are considered in making these decisions.

Tony will be allowed to be an elephant because the circus elephants are the first thing in which he has ever shown any interest. Greg has recently learned to turn somersaults and is very happy with his accomplishment, so we shall have him be one of the acrobats.

Nancy is not able to play the sandblocks in time because of a physical handicap, but she likes to play them, and she needs the exercise, so she will play in the band. Josephine is very shy and will not do anything that calls attention to herself; she will therefore sit with other children in the band and play sleighbells because she can do that without much effort.

Jim likes to ham it up and show off at every opportunity. We will therefore let him do something that gives him a chance to get some recognition, but we will not ask him to be the ringmaster since that would put him in view during most of the performance.

In similar fashion, a suitable part will be found for each child — not a part that makes for a better show, but one that is good for the child. When this has been done, the acts will be arranged in order. If programs are to be made, the children will make them as part of the unit work. The simplest kind of program is a booklet with one page for each act. A picture on each page lets the audience know what act comes next. If the programs are made by children who are able to write, each picture can be labeled and each page signed by those who appear in the act. The pages are then photocopied, collated, and assembled into booklets. An attractive cover may also be made for the programs.

Since several classes are going to work together, it is necessary to hold one or two rehearsals, partly because the children need to get used to the room and the arrangement of furniture and props and mostly because teachers have to learn where their groups will be seated, where equipment is to be placed, and when each child is to perform.

An appropriate song is sung or played as each act is performed. The songs given here are merely examples of very easy songs and should be changed or replaced to make them right for any particular group of children. The songs can be repeated as many times as necessary to accompany an act. By the time the unit is completed, even children who do not sing will usually have learned to recognize the music that accompanies each act.

RINGMASTER. Before the ringmaster announces the first number, the following song is sung. The ringmaster blows his whistle each time the children sing "blow."

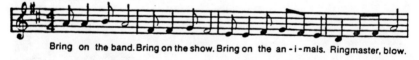

Bring on the band. Bring on the show. Bring on the an-i-mals. Ringmaster, blow.

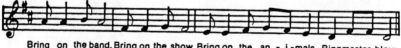

Bring on the band. Bring on the show. Bring on the an-i-mals. Ringmaster, blow.

BAND. The band plays one or or two lively pieces.

CLOWNS. The clowns do something they saw the circus clowns do, or they do some original thing that they think funny. The same song may be used for all the clown acts, or a different one can be sung to describe each one.

Funny, funny clowns. Funny, funny clowns. They make people laugh, Ha, ha, ha!

Funny, funny clowns. Funny, funny clowns. They make people laugh, Ha, ha, ha!

ELEPHANTS.

El - e - phants, el - e - phants. Great big, heav - y el - e - phants.

El - e - phants, el - e - phants. Sway, sway, sway.

ACROBATS.

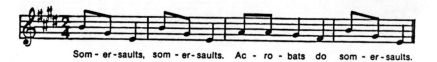

Som - er - saults, som - er - saults. Ac - ro - bats do som - er - saults.

Jump - ing on the tram - po - line, Jump, jump, jump.

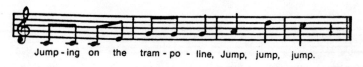

Jump - ing on the tram - po - line, Jump, jump, jump.

LIONS. The tamer directs the lions to their positions. Then, he has them roll on the floor or jump through hoops or whatever else they are going to do.

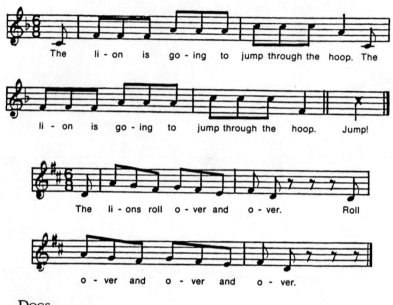

The li-on is go-ing to jump through the hoop. The

li-on is go-ing to jump through the hoop. Jump!

The li-ons roll o-ver and o-ver. Roll

o-ver and o-ver and o-ver.

Dogs.

The dogs stand up and dance a-round, dance a-round, dance around. The

dogs stand up and dance a-round. Dance a-round and round.

Acrobats. The tightrope walker walks on a balance beam or on a board set off the floor at a height comfortable for the child.

Tightrope walk-er, tightrope walk-er, Slow-ly, slow-ly, walk, walk, walk.

Tightrope walk-er, tightrope walk-er, Slow-ly, slow-ly, walk, walk, walk.

A swing or a swinging bar, or any other apparatus that sways back and forth, can be used as a trapeze.

Swing ing on the tra - peze. Swing ing on the tra - peze.

Swing - ing. Swing - ing. Swinging on the tra - peze.

HORSES.

Hors - es stepping, stepping high, Stepping, stepping, stepping high.

Galloping, galloping, galloping, galloping. Horses galloping 'round the ring.

VENDORS. Children carry food in shallow boxes. Boxes may be supported by straps hung around the children's necks. Money is collected in cans or boxes with slots in the top.

Hot dogs! Nice and hot! Hot dogs! Get them here!

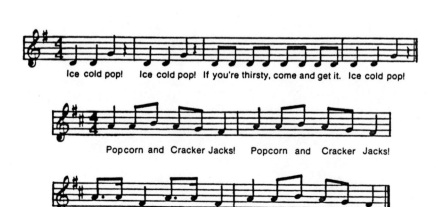

Ice cold pop! Ice cold pop! If you're thirsty, come and get it. Ice cold pop!

Popcorn and Cracker Jacks! Popcorn and Cracker Jacks!

Here you are. Here you are. Popcorn and Cracker Jacks!

Celebrations of special days can be planned in the same way if the holidays are treated as experience units. If the school has had a Christmas unit, for example, several classes can put on a program together, each class sharing its experiences with the others. Very young children who cannot sit still for long periods may want to have their own program with their guests.

In a class of young children, decorating a Christmas tree may have been the unit theme. This group might walk around a low platform with a small tree on it while they or the teachers sing, "Here we go 'round the Christmas tree." The children can take turns putting ornaments on the tree while the adults sing, "Cheryl is putting a star on the tree," or "Arthur is putting a bell on the tree."

Another class could show how they went to the store, selected gifts, and paid for them. The children would play the roles of customers, salesclerks, and cashier. Each part of the experience would have a song to go with it.

A third class may have made gifts, decorated paper and wrapped gifts in it, and tied ribbons. This class could act out the way they made the gifts and wrapping paper. They could then wrap the gifts and tie ribbons. Each of these processes could be described in a sequence song.

An advanced group that has done many things could arrange all their activities sequentially and present them with songs and other musical acts.

This kind of program is of value to the children because it makes sense to them. We need not worry about entertaining the audience; they will have a good time when they see the children enjoying themselves.

# BIBLIOGRAPHY

Alvin, J., *Music for the Handicapped Child* (2nd ed.). London: Oxford University Press, 1976.

Alvin, J., *Music Therapy*. New York: Basic Books, Inc., 1975.

Alvin, J., *Music Therapy for the Autistic Child*. New York: Oxford University Press, 1978.

Andrews, G., *Creative Rhythmic Movement for Children*. New York: Prentice-Hall, 1954.

Asimov, I., "One-to-One," in *Life and Time*. New York: Avon Books, 1978, pp. 193-201.

Baldwin, V.L., H.B. Bud Fredericks, and G. Brodsky, *Isn't it Time He Outgrew This?* Springfield, Illinois: Charles C Thomas, 1973.

Baumgartner, B.B., *Guiding the Retarded Child*. New York: John Day Co., 1965.

Beckwith, M., *So You Have to Teach Your Own Music*. West Nyack, New York: Parker Publishing Company, Inc., 1970.

Bell, P., *Basic Teaching for Slow Learners*. London: Muller Educational, 1970.

Bentley, W., *Learning to Move and Moving to Learn*. New York: Citation Press, 1970.

Blake, J.N., *Speech, Language and Learning Disorders*. Springfield, Illinois: Charles C Thomas, 1971.

Campbell, D.D., "One Out of Twenty: The LD," *Music Educators Journal*, Vol. 58, No. 8 (April 1972), pp. 38-39.

Carlson, B.W. and D.R. Gingland, *Play Activities for the Retarded Child*. Nashville, Tennessee: Abingdon Press, 1961.

Cruickshank, W.M., J.B. Junkala, and J.L. Paul, *The Preparation of Teachers of Brain-injured Children*. Syracuse, New York: Syracuse University Press, 1968.

D'Amelio, D., *Severely Retarded Children: Wider Horizons*. Columbus: Charles E. Merrill Publishing Company, 1971.

Darbes, A., "Music Therapy — A New Approach," *Music Therapy 1960*. Lawrence, Kansas: National Association for Music Therapy, Inc., 1961, pp. 20-23.

Deich, R.F. and P.M. Hodges, *Language without Speech*. New York: Brunner/Mazel, 1977.

Delp, H.A., "Three I's, Not the Three R's; a Philosophy for Teachers of Mentally Retarded," *The Training School Bulletin*, 55:11-14 (May 1958).

Dobbs, J.P.B., *The Slow Learner and Music*. London: Oxford University Press, 1966.

Drowatzky, J.N., *Physical Education for the Mentally Retarded*. Philadelphia: Lea and Febiger, 1971.

Elliott, R.N., Jr., "Mental Retardation," in *Humanistic Teaching for Exceptional Children*, ed. W.C. Morse. Syracuse, New York: Syracuse University Press, 1979, pp. 22-55.

Ellison, A., *Music with Children*. New York: McGraw-Hill Book Co., Inc., 1959.

Ewen, D., *Composers Since 1900*. New York: H.W. Wilson Co., 1969, pp. 394-398.

Flagg, M., "The Orff System in Today's World," *Music Educators Journal*, Vol. 53, No. 4 (Dec. 1966), p. 30.

Forman, G.E. and D.S. Kuschner, *The Child's Construction of Knowledge*. Monterey, California: Brooks/Cole Publishing Company, 1977.

Gearhart, B.R., *Learning Disabilities: Educational Strategies*. Saint Louis: The C.V. Mosby Company, 1973.

Giacobbe, G.A., "Rhythm Builds Order in Brain-Damaged Children," *Music Educators Journal*, Vol. 58, No. 8 (April 1972), pp. 40-42.

Gordon, T., *T.E.T. — Teacher Effectiveness Training*. New York: Peter H. Wyden, 1974.

Graham, R.M., "Seven Million Plus Need Special Attention. Who Are They?" *Music Educators Journal*, Vol. 58, No. 8 (April 1972), pp. 22-25+.

Graham, R.M. and A.S., *Teaching Music to the Exceptional Child*. Englewood Cliffs, N.J.: Prentice-Hall, Inc., 1980.

Greenberg, H.M., *Teaching with Feeling*. New York: Macmillan Company, 1969.

*Grove's Dictionary of Music and Musicians*. New York: St. Martin's Press, Inc., 1955, Vol. VI, pp. 281-282.

Harbert, W.K., *Opening Doors Through Music*. Springfield, Illinois: Charles C Thomas, 1974.

Haring, H.C., *Behavior of Exceptional Children*. Columbus: Charles E. Merrill, 1974.

Hawkinson, J. and M. Faulhaber, *Music and Instruments for Children to Make*. Chicago: Albert Whitman and Company, 1969.

Hickok, D. and J.A. Smith, *Creative Teaching of Music in the Elementary School*. Boston: Allyn and Bacon, Inc., 1974.

Hollander, H.C., *Creative Opportunities for the Retarded Child at Home and in School*. Garden City, New York: Doubleday and Company, 1971.

Hood, M.V., *Learning Music Through Rhythm*. Boston: Ginn and Company, 1949.

Hood, M.V., *Teaching Rhythm and Using Classroom Instruments*. Englewood Cliffs, N.J.: Prentice-Hall, Inc., 1970.

Hunter, H., *Growing up with Music*. Old Tappan, N.J.: Hewitt House, 1970.

Hunter, I. and M. Judson, *Simple Folk Instruments to Make and to Play*. New York: Simon and Schuster, 1977.

Hutt, M.L. and R.G. Gibby, *The Mentally Retarded Child*. Boston: Allyn and Bacon, Inc., 1965.

Hyatt, R. and N. Robnick, *Teaching the Mentally Handicapped Child*. New York: Behavioral Publications, Inc., 1974.

Ingram, C.P., *Education of the Slow-Learning Child* (3rd ed.). New York: The Ronald Press, 1960.

Isern, B., "The Influence of Music upon the Memory of Mentally Retarded Children," *Music Therapy 1958*. Lawrence, Kansas: National Association for Music Therapy, 1959, pp. 162-165.

Keetman, N.C., *Elementaria*. London: Schott and Co. Ltd., 1970.

Kephart, N.C., *The Slow Learner in the Classroom*. Columbus: Charles F. Merrill Books, Inc., 1960.

Kettelkamp, L., *Drums, Rattles, and Bells.* New York: William Morrow and Company, 1960.

Kirk, S.A., *Educating Exceptional Children* (2nd ed.). Boston: Houghton Mifflin Company, 1972.

Kirk, S.A., *You and Your Retarded Child.* New York: Macmillan Company, 1955.

Koch, R., and K.J. Koch, *Understanding the Mentally Retarded Child.* New York: Random House, 1974.

Landis, B. and P. Carder, *The Eclectic Curriculum in American Music Education: Contributions of Dalcroze, Kodaly, and Orff.* Washington, D.C.: Music Educators National Conference, 1972.

Levin, H.D. and G.M. Levin, "Instrumental Music: A Great Ally in Promoting Self-Image," *Music Educators Journal,* Vol. 58, No. 8 (April 1972), pp. 31-34.

Madsen, C.K. and C.H. Madsen, Jr., *Experimental Research in Music.* Englewood Cliffs, N.J.: Prentice-Hall, 1970.

Mandell, M. and R.E. Wood, *Make Your Own Musical Instruments.* New York: Sterling Publishing Co., Inc., 1957.

Mark, M.L., *Contemporary Music Education.* New York: Schirmer Books, 1978.

McMillan, L.E., *Guiding Children's Growth Through Music.* Boston: Ginn and Company, 1959.

Meyen, E.L. *Developing Units of Instruction: for the Mentally Retarded and Other Children with Learning Problems.* Dubuque, Iowa: William C. Brown Company, 1972.

Mursell, J.L., *Education for Musical Growth.* Boston: Ginn and Company, 1948.

Mursell, J.L., *Human Values in Music Education.* New York: Silver, Burdett and Company, 1934.

Mursell, J.L., *Music and the Classroom Teacher.* New York: Silver Burdett Company, 1951.

Neff, H. and J. Pilch, *Teaching Handicapped Children Easily.* Springfield, Illinois: Charles C Thomas, 1976.

Nicholls, H. and A., *Creative Teaching.* London: George Allen & Unwin Ltd., 1975.

Nichtern, S., *Helping the Retarded Child.* New York: Grosset & Dunlap, 1974.

Nocera, S.D., "Special Education Teachers Need a Special Education," *Music Educators Journal,* Vol. 58, No. 8 (April 1972), pp. 73-75.

Nordoff, P. and C. Robbins, *Music Therapy in Special Education.* New York: John Day Company, 1971.

Nordoff, P. and C. Robbins, *Therapy in Music for Handicapped Children.* New York: St. Martin's Press, 1971.

Nye, R.E. and V.T. Nye, *Music in the Elementary School* (3rd ed.). Englewood Cliffs, N.J.: Prentice-Hall, 1970.

Perry, N., *Teaching the Mentally Retarded Child* (2nd ed.). New York: Columbia University Press, 1974.

Podolsky, E., *Music Therapy.* New York: Philosophical Library, 1954.

Portnoy, J., *Music in the Life of Man.* New York: Holt, Rinehart and Winston, 1963.

Radler, D.H. with N.C. Kephart, *Success through Play.* New York: Harper and Brothers, 1960.

Robins, F. and J., *Educational Rhythmics for Mentally Handicapped Children.* New York: Horizon Press Publishers, 1965.

Robison, D.E., "There's Therapy in Rhythm," *Music Educators Journal,* Vol. 57, No. 7 (March 1971), pp. 42-44, 95-100.

Rothman, E.P., *Troubled Teachers.* New York: David McKay Company, Inc., 1977.

Rothstein, J.H., *Mental Retardation: Readings and Resources* (2nd ed.). New York: Holt, Rinehart and Winston, Inc., 1971.

Runkle, A. and M.L. Eriksen, *Music for Today's Boys and Girls.* Boston: Allyn and Bacon, Inc., 1970.

Sheehy, E.D., *Children Discover Music and Dance.* New York: Henry Holt and Company, Inc., 1959.

Smith, R.M., *Clinical Teaching* (2nd ed.). New York: McGraw-Hill, 1974.

Tagatz, G.E., *Child Development and Individually Guided Education.* Reading, Massachusetts: Addison-Wesley Publishing Company, 1976.

Thorpe, L.P. *Child Psychology and Development.* New York: Ronald Press Co., 1955.

Turton, L.J., "Preschool Language Disabilities," in *Humanistic Teaching for Exceptional Children,* ed. W.C. Morse. Syracuse, N.Y.: Syracuse University Press, 1979, pp. 151-176.

Van Riper, C., *Speech Correction* (4th ed.). Englewood Cliffs, N.J.: Prentice-Hall, Inc., 1963.

Van Riper, C., *Teaching Your Child to Talk.* New York: Harper and Brothers, 1950.

Van Riper, C., *Your Child's Speech Problems.* New York: Harper and Brothers, 1961.

Wallin, J.E.W., *Education of Mentally Handicapped Children.* New York: Harper and Brothers, 1955.

Weber, E.W., *Mentally Retarded Children and Their Education.* Springfield, Illinois: Charles C Thomas, 1963.

Williams, W., L. Brown, and N. Certo, "Basic Components of Instructional Programs," in *Educating the Severely and Profoundly Retarded,* ed. R.M. Anderson. Baltimore: University Park Press, 1976, pp. 55-74.

# INDEX

# INDEX OF MUSICAL EXAMPLES